Somewhere round the corner

For Chris and Mike

Somewhere round the corner

Jenny Green

With Best wishes,

Jenny.

TWELVE ACRE PUBLISHING

© Jenny Green, 2014

First published in 2014 by
Twelve Acre Publishing
Lynaica
Barline
Beer
East Devon EX12 3LR

www.twelveacrepublishing.co.uk

ISBN 978-0-9555902-1-4

British Library Cataloguing in Publication Data
is available from the British Library

The rights of Jenny Green to be identified as author of this work has been asserted in accordance with the Copyright Designs and Patents Act 1988

All rights reserved. No part of this publication may be reproduced, stored in a retrieval system, or transmitted, in any form or by any means, electronic, mechanical, photocopying, recording or otherwise, without the prior permission of the publisher.

Printed in UK by Russell Press Ltd, Nottingham

For Lawrence
and in memory of
my parents Jack and Trudie Green

with special thanks to Barbara Bleiman

FAMILY & RELATIVES WHO APPEAR IN THE BOOK

Trudie's family

Landsboroughs
Father: Thomas Landsborough 'Dads'
Mother: Gertrude Pearce Landsborough – 'Mumsie'
Sister: Susie Landsborough – 'Toozle'
Brother: Alex Landsborough and wife Kathleen
Brother: Henry Landsborough and wife Peggy
Nieces: Elizabeth, Susan, and Jane (Peggy and Henry's daughters)
Cousin: Willie Landsborough (Thomas's cousin)
Cousin: Gordon Landsborough (Trudie's second cousin)
Gordon's children: Bonny and Stuart (who Trudie never knew)

Pearces
Uncles: Henry and Earnest (Jewellers in Huddersfield), Charlton in Wanganui, John in Perth
Aunts: Emily (Chiswick), Marie (Newton Abbot), Win (Charlton's wife), Alice (John's wife)
Cousins: Nancie (sees Trudie off), Dick and Isabel (Perth), Girlie (Wanganui), May (daughter of Ernest and Anne – for whom Trudie is a bridesmaid)

Jack's Family

The Greens & Lawrances
Father: Syd Green
Mother: Annie Green née Lawrance
Mother's cousin: Helen Lawrance
Aunt: Winnie Lawrance
Brother: Sydney Green
Son: Peter Green
Daughter: Jennifer (Jenny) Green
Nephew: Mike Green

CONTENTS

Family & Relatives who appear in the book		vi
Chapter 1	On the Orient line	1
Chapter 2	Ceylon Tea	24
Chapter 3	Into the Forest	43
Chapter 4	The Great Southern	76
Chapter 5	The Traveller and the Genie	105
Chapter 6	Otago	126
Chapter 7	Tracking and Trekking	146
Chapter 8	Puzzling World	160
Chapter 9	Family Silver	179
Chapter 10	No Name	194
Chapter 11	Harbours	214
Chapter 12	Home	239
Chapter 13	Hartrigg House	260
Chapter 14	Memory	283
Acknowledgements		290

CHAPTER 1 – On the Orient Line

I HAVE SO LITTLE LEFT OF MY MOTHER, who died when I was nine. I had spent those years following her death storing up every possible memory of her as her possessions gradually disappeared. Not at first: to begin with her things were everywhere in the house. I'd feel in the pockets of her green coat, left hanging in the passage, and find a hankie that still smelled of her. I'd go to her sewing box and play with the thimbles. I'd climb up to the attic, where all the treasures from her journey round the world were stored and I'd reach for my favourites: a porcupine quill, a stuffed duck-billed platypus and a little pile of polished wood. I'd take them out carefully from the cabinet just as she had told me to do. Back down one flight of stairs, in my parents' bedroom, I'd touch the black velvet evening dress that my mother rarely wore. I'd hold her red wedding dress against me as I stared at my reflection in the wardrobe mirror. I'd carefully open her jewellery box and try on her pearl necklace. I'd stare at the pictures on the mantelpiece: the coloured photograph of Pango Pango, the black and white photograph of Mummy and Daddy paddling in the sea. 'You were still somewhere round the corner then,' she would say when I asked her where I was. I could never quite imagine Mummy and Daddy without me. After her death I found it hard to understand that there was no 'Mummy'. I tried to memorise every story she had told me and keep safe every treasure she had left behind.

The things I have now, fifty years on, I can itemise in a few lines:

> an address book
> a boomerang
> a diamond ring
> a gold watch (no longer working)
> a red crêpe wedding dress.

There is also an old photograph album, which arrived in a parcel from my cousin Susan at the beginning of 2006 with this covering letter:

Dearest Jennifer
I enclose these albums for you. I found them when finally sorting out Mum's stuff. Thought you might like some of the family photographs etc.
   Hopefully see you soon,
   Lots of love,
   Sue

I looked through the first album. The pictures were tiny black and white or brown and white photographs of dead relatives. Ghosts. I wrapped the albums back in the brown paper parcel and put them into 'Pandora's Box'. It's my name for the trunk where I keep my family stuff, hidden but not thrown out.

The following summer the trunk had to be sorted because we were letting our house. We were going back to Lawrence's home in Trinidad. He had been given a three-year research post at the University of Trinidad and Tobago to work on the background to his new novel. We had not lived there since 1990. All our possessions had to be organised: unnecessary items thrown out, the rest stored in the back bedroom. I had left Pandora until the very end, reluctant to go back into my past when so many exciting things were happening right now. As I opened the lid, the first thing I saw, at the very top, was the brown paper parcel. I had forgotten about it. I pulled out the albums and this time picked the one at the bottom – an antique folder with that damp, musty smell of old things. The front cover had gone, it was just black paper, but bits of blue card remained on the spine and a sad-looking tassel of faded red and gold cord still hung from the back. I opened it and discovered not photographs but letters. The first letter was stuck in its pale blue envelope on to the first page. The handwriting looked vaguely familiar. I carefully pulled out the letter so I didn't damage the envelope.

I read the printed heading: 'Orient Line, SS *Oronsay*'. The letter must be from my mother! It was dated 18 December, 5 p.m. I knew the year. I didn't need any verification from the postmark. It was 1937. This was the first letter my mother wrote home on her year's visit to Australia as a Commonwealth exchange teacher.

My cousin Sue had discovered a treasure trove and I had just bunged it into the trunk. I rang her immediately. She hadn't discovered the letters either. Then I read them all. I was transported to Western Australia of 1938 by my mother's young voice. I wanted to set off there immediately to find her, but I was about to travel east to Trinidad, the wrong way round

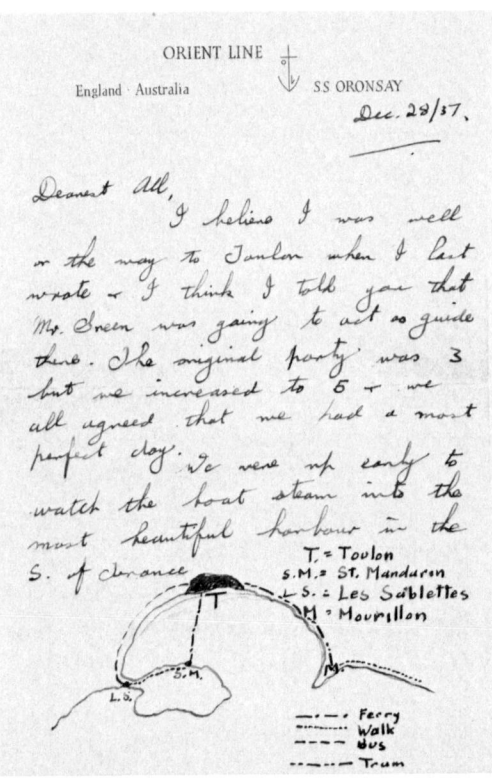

the world. So instead I packed up the letters and took them to Trinidad with me, along with my father's letters, which I had rescued from the clear-out of the old house in Shrewsbury and then saved from his flat after he died back in 1975. I hadn't read them in a long time.

*

It's 2 December 2010, the coldest day of the year so far, and after three years in Trinidad neither Lawrence nor I are prepared for this. We do our final check before we get into the taxi: passports, tickets, money, credit cards, mobiles, itinerary and address books. As I look at my passport under the name 'Scott' and my driver's licence under 'Green' I begin to panic, although it's never yet caused a problem. I'm overwhelmed by anxiety, even though I'm quite used to travelling. There have been many departures, I know the routine, but this journey is different. It's not just a holiday or a return trip home to Trinidad. This is the journey that I've been waiting to do for a lifetime. Now Lawrence's research is complete and his novel is more or less finished, it is my turn for discovery. This is my research, my quest for the lives of my parents. I'm terrified that something will go wrong and our months of planning will come to nothing. I've been listening to weather forecasts on television and on the radio, and this morning I've checked online before hiding my laptop away. Snow is forecast, more thick snow. Gatwick has already closed and Heathrow is under threat.

I put on the burglar alarm, lock up carefully and Lawrence waves goodbye to our mythical house guest. We're on our way across a silent, dark, snowy London towards Heathrow.

As we turn off the A40 on to the A312 I can see planes taking off. We look at each other and smile. The taxi finally draws up at Terminal 3. We rush to the first monitor we see as we arrive. All flights are scheduled. There it is: 'Singapore Airlines Flight 297'. Under Departures I read 'on time'.

Relief is the only word for it now that we've checked in our bags, cleared security, made sure once again that our plane really is there on the monitor and settled down to breakfast in Chez Gerard. I dig in my bag for the folder of photocopied letters. Yes, they are here, all in order, the ones on the top written on the SS *Oronsay*.

*

S.S. Oronsay.

It was bitterly cold too when Trudie set off from Tilbury aboard the *Oronsay* on 18 December 1937. She was twenty-six years old, nearly twenty-seven. She wrote her first letter home to 'Dads' at 5 p.m. that day. The postmark is 'Brixham'.

Dearest Dads,
Very many thanks for your lovely letter and the telegram which was waiting for me on board. I'm really truly off now, on my way to the other side of the world. I can hardly believe it. We left Auntie Emily's at Chiswick early this morning to get to the boat train from St Pancras. It was quite a long run to Tilbury and oh so cold. Mother,

Susie and Cousin Nancie came to see me off. Before the boat started we all got terribly cold waiting to wave goodbye. It was about twelve I think when she started and when I could no longer see Susie, who had of course got to the very far point of the wharf, I went down below to get warm.

And she wrote to her mother, who was staying on with her sister, Auntie Emily, in Chiswick:

Dearest Mumsie,
I do hope none of you caught cold while waiting this morning. I was glad of a hot lunch at 12.30. I'm relieved to say that all the exchange teachers are not on the same table though they are fairly close. There are three of the profession at my table including myself but the other two are both men. Mr Holmes, the one you saw on the train, and the other one is the one you saw me smiling at just as you were going off the boat. He's rather nice – a modern languages teacher.

When Trudie got back below to her cabin she was hoping to snuggle into her bunk to warm up and have a little weep. She would miss Susie so much, as well as Dads and Mumsie. However, she was greeted by Miss Petyt, her cabin mate. Miss Petyt, who was also on exchange, was going to New Zealand. They discovered that they were both from Yorkshire and also keen hikers and climbers. 'Most of my luggage is a rucksack, climbing boots and a tent,' confessed Miss Petyt. 'I hope we won't need too many formal frocks on board.' There was hardly time to introduce themselves and make small talk before the gong sounded for lunch. Trudie braced herself to meet more new people. She rather hoped she wouldn't be put on a large table full of exchange teachers.

There were only three of them at the table laid for four. The other two were men, both of them exchange teachers bound for New Zealand. Over lunch they discussed the journey. The men seemed very knowledgeable. Mr Green already knew Toulon, their second stop. He was a French master and had travelled frequently in France, especially along the Riviera. Trudie was amused at the way he used French mannerisms as he flourished his French vocabulary. Mr Holmes taught classics. Trudie thought she could have guessed their subjects by their personalities. Green seemed the romantic type and Holmes the pedant. Mr Green promised to show them his version of Toulon, 'where the tourists won't go and we can eat real French *cuisine* for half the price'. Not to be beaten, Mr Holmes promised them his expertise when they reached Pompeii. 'I can show you the very best views from the ruins,' he offered.

That first night Trudie couldn't sleep, despite being exhausted. Too much had happened and she hadn't yet got used to the rolling of the boat, and still she had the Bay of Biscay to come. She hadn't eaten much at dinner and was amazed at the quantities the two men had put away. Nor did she feel she had fully held her own in the conversation about books. The men had rattled off authors and poets as if they were their personal friends. She hoped she had not made a complete fool of herself when she had quoted a few verses from Robbie Burns in her best Scottish accent. She smiled to herself now, as she knew these southerners couldn't tell the difference between Highland and Dumfriesshire vowels. Dads 'wudda bin that proud a his own wee lassie'.

And so her journey began. I imagine her sleeping there in her cabin as the ship passed along the English coast, landing the pilot at Brixham at 7.30 the next morning. It was rough crossing the Bay of Biscay. Trudie wrote: *I'm afraid I did not get through the Bay of Biscay well, I had to retire to my cabin and lie down. I fed on biscuits and raisins for two days thanks to Susie's thoughtfulness.*

But the weather got warmer and the sea grew calmer off the Portuguese coast. Trudie enjoyed the games of deck quoits and her walks round the ship with her (unnamed) table companion.

At Gibraltar, where the sun was hot for their brief visit ashore, she described her impressions: *The streets of the town are narrow and very steep. The main road is lined with bazaars with handsome young Spaniards tempting one to buy their wares for 'nearly nothing'. I was so excited to see the oranges growing on the hillside I wanted to reach out and pick them.*

She completed this letter home just before reaching Toulon, ending with: *By the way I'm becoming terribly high-brow and getting quite expert at discussing modern literature.* I can see my father at the dinner table holding forth on poetry. Is it Trudie or Holmes that he is aiming to impress? There are my parents sitting at dinner together on that first evening as they set sail out on this voyage across the world.

Jack's first letter home, though brief, offers an

interesting comparison to Trudie's three letters. To him the Bay of Biscay was *comparatively calm and our boat took it marvellously and I felt hungry all the time.* His view of Gibraltar was of *a very ugly barren barrack-ridden sort of place. There was a black mist hanging over the rock so you couldn't see the top; the air was warm and oppressive.* He enjoys life on board, especially the deck quoits, the dancing and the food. Sadly, there is no mention of who he plays deck quoits with or who partners him for dancing. He gives a brief comment on Spain: *we are giving the Spanish waters a very wide berth so there is little likelihood of encountering the horrors that are going on there with Franco and his fascist friends.* This is the touch of Jack that I knew, a man committed to fighting oppression.

Trudie was thrilled at her first sighting of Toulon, her first view of the South of France on Christmas Eve 1937. She was up at dawn to watch the boat steam into what was described in the guidebook as 'the most beautiful harbour in the South of France.' There it was, surrounded by high peaks with bare limestone tops alight in the sun. The lower slopes were tree-clad, a shimmering deep green. The bay was full of gunboats, but the rows of washing hanging on the decks made them look less menacing. Jack and Holmes had asked her to join them for the day. She had caught in Jack's tone his excitement at coming back to a part of the world that he loved. He was a strange chap, she thought, sometimes so distant, so distracted, hardly listening to a word she said, yet at other times animated, amusing, kind. He had quickly asked her to call him

Jack; he hated formality, he said. But Holmes had remained Holmes. He was less attractive in both personality and looks. Although he couldn't be much older than her, everything about him seemed middle-aged.

The tender arrived to take them ashore at ten. Their group was joined by Bridget, Trudie's new friend, who was also on the Australian exchange, and Margaret Petyt. Trudie felt mildly disappointed, as she'd looked on this as a chance to get to know Jack a little more. After the group had changed their pounds into francs, he suggested they take the ferry across to St Mandarin.

'This is what the locals do,' he said. 'I'm going to show you the secret beauties of Toulon today.'

They were cramped in the little ferry full of fisher-wives and their children who'd been into Toulon to do their last bits of shopping before Christmas. They were carrying huge bags and baskets of vegetables of all kinds, some very strange, Trudie thought. She noticed the thin loaves, yards long, tucked under their arms or sticking out of their bags. The locals rushed out of the boat at St Mandarin with all the confidence of people who do it every day. The English group slowly disembarked, amazed by the simplicity yet beauty of the little fishing village.

'Look at all the green shutters of the cottages,' Trudie said. 'They are all matching, and match the fishing boats too.'

'Not all,' corrected Holmes. 'Some of the boats are blue and pink.' He pointed at the harbour, where huge quantities of nets were drying in the sun.

Jack guided them to a little path which climbed the

hills along the coast towards the bathing beach of Les Sablettes.

'Doesn't he speak French like a native and he knows all the nooks and crannies,' commented Bridget. 'That's what comes of being a modern languages teacher; you get to know the host country and the language so well.' Trudie felt it was something more, but she couldn't put her finger on it; it was almost as if he changed personality when he spoke French. She knew she'd not experiment with her mediocre French, with an English accent, in front of him.

The hillside was covered with aromatic shrubs. There were sage and thyme and other herbs that Trudie didn't recognise. She wasn't sure what the large bushes with the red berries were and made a note to ask Jack. She loved the smell of the Mediterranean pine. The views of the bays below and the mountains above were thrilling, just so different from anything she'd seen before. Jack pointed out large châteaux, a casino and a monastery. They climbed down to the deserted beach, Les Sablettes, which apparently was crowded in summer. It was too chilly now even for a paddle, but they collected some shells and inspected a washed-up porpoise that was still alive. Then, realising that they were all starving, they found the bus stop just at the end of the stretch of sand and caught a bus that took them back to the centre of Toulon. Jack said he knew of a perfect little restaurant between the port and the station where the locals said you got good value for money.

Trudie had never tasted food like this before. On her skiing trip to Switzerland she remembered the food as a little stodgy. It was fun working out the menu, with the help of Holmes and Jack. They all had the thick vegetable soup to start. Jack recommended the aioli with fish and vegetables as an entrée, but Trudie didn't fancy tasting garlic all day so she chose the champignons. She got rather confused when they brought the main course, coq au vin with lettuce, before the vegetables. She hardly had room left for the creamed spinach, sauté potatoes and stuffed tomatoes. When the dessert of pears and ice cream arrived she realised they had been eating for two hours! 'Totally normal,' Jack announced. 'The French value food, unlike us.' Trudie didn't voice her disagreement, but she knew in her home how Sunday roast with Yorkshire was highly valued, a ritual never missed, and the meat the staple for the rest of the week.

Everyone felt sleepy after the meal, but Jack assured them that Mourillon was definitely worth a visit and they could nod off on the tram. Trudie was wide awake again as they hurtled along the narrow streets, waiting at loops when a tram coming from the opposite direction appeared. With its pretty, enclosed beach and scattering of rocks in the sea, Mourillon was as lovely as Jack had suggested. Trudie thought how perfect it would be to visit in late summer, when the sea would be at its warmest and you could eat outside at the little café. They climbed up steep steps to the path cut out of the side of the cliff with views of the coast: pink cliffs, blue sea and sky, bright green-topped pines with pinkish trunks all lit by the setting sun. This was the highlight. She noticed how the group fell silent as they walked, awed by the beauty. She turned to thank Jack for bringing them all here, but he too seemed lost in his own thoughts.

The evening in Toulon was equally magical. While most of the group went shopping for souvenirs, Trudie found herself wandering through the backstreets near the port, chaperoned by Jack. He hated shopping, he'd said, and she didn't want to spend any of her small budget at this stage. He described his favourite places along the whole southern coast of France and she listened entranced. What a sheltered life she'd led, she thought. She only had her skiing trip with Susie in Switzerland to offer.

They checked out a few possible restaurants for supper, then wandered into the brightly lit cathedral and Trudie inspected the crib. Jack was more interested in the architecture; he wasn't a believer, he'd explained. It was so different from church at home, where people would be singing carols. There were many on their knees silently praying and the smell of incense permeated the interior. Trudie felt a sudden pang for Highfield Congregational. Here, in the cathedral, they met the rest of the group and Jack became the guide again, leading them to a little restaurant where he thought the menu looked reasonable yet interesting. There were still more surprises. Trudie ate fresh anchovies for the first time and huge globe artichokes. She copied those who knew how to pick and dip the leaves in the sauce.

After a final coffee the tender picked them up at 10.30. The group sang 'For he's a jolly good fellow' to Jack as they headed back to the ship. Everyone realised how much money he had saved them. The whole cost of this trip was about six shillings, including two brilliant meals, whereas the ship's tour cost seventeen shillings and sixpence. And what a day it had been, right off the beaten track to places they would never have seen otherwise. 'My turn when we reach Pompeii,' Holmes reminded them. 'I'll do you the honours there.' Trudie smiled to herself. She was always amused at the way men got competitive.

As she was lying in her bunk with images of the wonderful day floating through her mind, Margaret suddenly said, 'That Mr Green, he seems to have taken a shine to you!'

Trudie felt herself blush and was glad it was dark. 'I don't think so,' she said quietly. She pictured his intense blue eyes and how they sometimes looked at her without really seeing her.

Jack was lying on his bunk, while his young cabin mate, Dick, in the bunk above was gently snoring. Jack couldn't sleep. He was thinking of his last visit here with Joyce. It had been early August 1936, about eighteen months ago, before she finally told him that things were over. They had taken a ten-day holiday together. He had been thrilled and excited when she agreed. He had thought it was a sign of acceptance, at last. He'd booked the Grand Hotel at Le Trayas on the Esterelle coast, not far from Cannes. The hotel was new and built rather like a liner, jutting out into the sea among the red rocks, in what they call the Deco style. It was the most luxurious hotel he'd ever stayed in, but it was where he intended to propose, again. She had agreed to share a room and he had taken this as a sign that now, after all the years he had loved her, she really intended to agree to marriage.

The day in Toulon had been her suggestion. They'd caught the train along the coast and had intended to do the very walk he had guided the party along today. He had imagined proposing to her on a cliffside overlooking the Mediterranean, taking her in his arms, thinking at last that she would be his. But it hadn't happened. Joyce had gone cold on him, as she so often had. The night before, when they'd made love, he had had a premonition. She was there, but not there. He had little intimate experience of other women, but he felt she did not truly enjoy love. As they began the walk from Mourillon, almost as if she had read his mind, guessed his intentions, she had picked a quarrel. He had risen to the bait. She had accused him of being a dilettante, of not getting down to anything serious, of drifting. 'You'll never be a writer, Jack,' she had said. 'You've got nothing original to say, and despite what you think, you've never really suffered.' He had said cruel things too, accused her of not being womanly, of being frigid. He had even been sarcastic about her poetry. He hated to think now of what he had said. That moment had been the beginning of the end. They'd returned to the station and caught the train back to Le Trayas without speaking. Gradually, over the next few days, they had made it up. He was relieved that she'd not just got the next train home. Perhaps she had felt that his love and friendship of so many years were of some value, though she had made sure she had slept in the other bed. He had never made love to her again, although he had continued to see her. She was still his friend. He understood more about her now. She had at least, eventually, been completely honest with him. He had wanted to lay the ghost today, to say to himself, it is over, she's gone and I'm free at last. But he wasn't sure if this was true.

*

The flight on Singapore Airlines is very smooth. I have spent the time rereading all the early letters and marking the places we'll visit in Sri Lanka. I put them away. The one from Jack to his parents from Le Trayas dated 8 August 1936 intrigues me. What did my grandparents think of his holidaying with his ladyfriend, Joyce? He was twenty-eight by then and I imagine they were hoping he would settle down. Did they approve, though, of this relationship? He had met her at university, so it had been going a while without an 'outcome'. I rack my brains to remember the little snippets Dad had told me about Joyce. Whatever became of that book of her poetry he had treasured? What a pity I don't know her full name. I dig in my rucksack for my mother's little address book, remembering that I've seen a Joyce. Here it is, in pencil. I can just read: Miss Joyce Baker, Kainga, Maldon Road, Wroughton, Nr Swindon, Wilts. But it's not really very likely that Trudie would have *this* Joyce's address.

Our visit to Singapore is brief, a day, a night and a day. It's a good place to recover from jet lag and relax. The weather is sunny and warm and we have that smugness of travellers who know they've left winter behind. On our second day we visit Raffles. In the hotel's museum we look at photographs and mementoes of all the celebrities who have spent time here. I discover Somerset Maugham. There are photographs of him in the bar, in the dining room, in the magnificent courtyard. And there is a collection of first editions of all his novels. I recognise not only the titles of books but the colours and shapes of the copies I have at home: *The Narrow Corner*, *The Moon and Sixpence*, *Cakes and Ale*, *Of Human Bondage*, *The Summing Up*.

'I wonder if mine are first editions,' I say to Lawrence. 'He was Dad's favourite writer and I think I have every novel he wrote.'

We have caffè lattes rather than gin slings in the famous bar where the stars of the past frolicked and the tourists of today hang out. I tell Lawrence how my father encouraged me to read Maugham when I was seventeen. I was applying to university to study English and had read only the literature we'd covered at school and a few classics, Austen and the Brontës. I was an avid consumer of romance and crime, so I asked my father what I should try to build up my serious reading and he suggested Somerset Maugham. I read *The Narrow Corner*, which I much preferred to *Lord Jim*, our A-level text, which had a similar setting. However, my teacher, Miss Cooper, was not impressed. 'Somerset Maugham? You must do some substantial reading, Jennifer, if you really want to read English at university.' I mimic her voice. 'Guess what?' I continue. 'The next day she brought me a pile of Thomas Hardy novels. So, you see, that was the end of Maugham for me.'

'You must read them,' Lawrence insists. 'Perhaps you'll find some clues to your father. They may have some notes or cuttings in them, provided you can find them.' He laughs. The lack of order in Lawrence's study, where all our books are shelved, is a standing joke.

'They should be on one of the shelves by the door,' I say, as I picture those grey-green hardback covers. 'I wish I'd checked them out before.'

I'm so different from Lawrence in that way. He is forever searching through old books, looking at old photographs, and he has used his family memorabilia throughout his writing. Family photographs litter his study and small artefacts from home in Trinidad sit on his study mantelpiece – his father's shaving bowl, his mother's rosary – whereas I have shut everything away in the trunk.

After the morning spent in Raffles, where we feel as if we've been in 'time past', we wander out into the modern streets. While some of the city reminds us of Port of Spain, where we lived in Trinidad, especially the modernity and colonial side by side, it seems much cleaner, much more organised, and not nearly as exciting. Yet it is an ideal place to recover from jet lag before we take off again this evening at midnight. We'll be in Sri Lanka by 2 a.m. Sri Lankan time – the magic of fast flight and time change.

*

The *Oronsay* was moving rather more slowly. The exchange teachers and the rest of the passengers on board had Christmas Day at sea. Deck games were organised, a traditional Christmas dinner and dancing. Two days later, after visiting Pompeii and Naples, Jack wrote to his parents:

SS *Oronsay*, 28 Dec. 1937

Dear Mum and Dad

Just a line to let you know how I'm getting on. Toulon was lovely; the huge harbour is encircled by pine clad hills, and behind there is a wall of barren mountains. The battle ships, ironically beautiful things despite their ugly purpose, looked ghastly in the morning mist.

We explored the coast both sides of the town and did that lovely cliff walk I knew which is equal to anything in the more popular stretches of the Riviera. It was a lovely warm sunny day; you could not believe it was Christmas Eve. We lunched and dined at typical French restaurants and tasted the Provençal delicacies. I was very thrilled by Aioli, a thick garlic mayonnaise eaten with boiled fish and vegetables. We had a truly grand day and came back to the boat at midnight.

I'm both amused and irritated by his lack of detail about people, especially compared to Trudie's letters. Not a person is mentioned by name. His highlight appears to be the aioli! His description of Christmas is equally brief: *Xmas was quite jolly on board, but quite*

unremarkable. We danced until midnight.

I wonder about the 'We'. How many dances did he have with Trudie?

The letter ends with their last stop in the Mediterranean before they reach the Suez Canal:

We had a drive to Pompeii. I was surprised by the beauty and extent of this ruined city. The sky was grey as we left Naples and looked towards the shore. Vesuvius appeared snow-capped above the hard black lower slopes. It was a magnificent study in black and white. Then we passed Stromboli, that great active volcano on a lone inhabited island. It spat flames and sparks into the night and you could see the molten lava pouring down its slopes. Tomorrow we arrive in Port Said. I'm sorry that we are parting with quite a number of interesting passengers. Many migrating peoples got on at Naples, escaping from Fascism to wherever they can get to. The ones that can afford to, or are able to, of course.

Trudie's last letter from this leg of the journey is written when they have just left Aden to cross the Indian Ocean to Ceylon:

6/1/38

Dear All,
It is amazing how the days fly past and the letters just don't get written. We've had rather disappointing weather since Naples which was rather a shame: 'See Naples and die of cold' was my description of that magnificent bay backed by the ever smoking Vesuvius. It was a dull

morning with no sun and a bitterly cold wind when we disembarked and we were glad to get into coaches as quickly as possible to go to Pompeii. We travelled along one of the new and much boasted Italian roads. Rather ugly I thought. However the old boys who built Pompeii certainly had an eye for beauty, looking along many of the roads you get a perfect picture of Vesuvius and looking the other way you see fold upon fold of the Apennines disappearing into clouds. It is rather 'un worldly', the roads, temples, garden, and houses, so well preserved. I would have loved to have explored the town on my own or with a friend. Going in a full group and having two guides, the official one and Holmes, rather took the atmosphere away and now it seems a long time ago that I was there, further back than Toulon, or Gibraltar, or even Tilbury.

Like Jack, she comments on the refugees: *At Naples many emigrants embarked fleeing Europe, well over a hundred Italians, Yugo-Slavs, Germans and Poles: a harsh reminder of present times. No wonder we have twenty two nationalities on board.* And she is thrilled by the fact of leaving Europe: *In Port Said we were definitely away from Europe and there seemed to be an air of intrigue and excitement about everything.* But, unlike Jack, she provides much more comment on the social aspects of the journey:

So much for our ports of call. The days in between are just one round of enjoyment eating and sleeping and talking. There are some interesting folks on board but its rather strange that all going out on exchange were determined to have as little as possible to do with the other teachers yet we have gradually gravitated towards each other. I'm particularly friendly with Bridget, a girl from York who teaches in London. Holmes and Green are very good at looking after the whole party but when we are ashore we split into smaller groups and us four stick together. And as for dancing Bridget and I tend to get the two men to ourselves. We have nick-named Mr Green 'Brother Jack' as he has strong left wing leanings. Not the same politics as you, Dads, but you would find him interesting. As well as teaching French and German he plans to be a writer. In Colombo we have booked a car for 6 to go to Kandy – the four of us, a laddie of 17 from Green's cabin and Margaret from mine. I can't wait to see Ceylon. Our itinerary, which is just for one day ashore, includes spice gardens, temples, and tea-plantations. I can't believe I'm on my way to a tropical island!

Trudie's passport photo taken 1935

CHAPTER 2 – Ceylon Tea

'CEYLON TEA IS THE VERY BEST TEA,' my mother would say as she poured my cup out when we got home. It was that hour of special time before my brother and father got back, just us drinking our Ceylon tea and my mother listening to me as I described my day at Stepping Stones School. We'd sit at the kitchen table, a checked seersucker cloth, the pale green teapot, milk jug and sugar basin, and cups and saucers to match. There's a little plate with carefully counted out Cadbury's chocolate fingers. And there's the tea strainer, of course, sitting on its own saucer. It is much more difficult to picture my mother, to actually remember her face.

*

We are going backwards in time as we cross the Bay of Bengal from Singapore to Sri Lanka. I am going backwards in time trying to discover Jack and Trudie on their SS *Oronsay* voyage. They had crossed the Arabian Ocean and the Indian Ocean, and had disembarked in Ceylon, at the harbour near Pettah, close to the heart of the old city of Colombo.

Our plane arrives on time at Bandaranaike International Airport, thirty kilometres north of Colombo. Is it two or four o'clock in the morning? It's two o'clock, so we are back where we began. The airport is packed. It reminds me of arriving in Trinidad: the noise, the smells of perfume mixed with sweat, the heat and the huge queues at Immigration. We finally reach Arrivals, where there's lots of shouting: between friends, from porters hurrying past and families greeting each other. Everyone seems to know where they are going, except us. What a relief to find our guides with a big sign: 'Butterfly Holidays'. Athula and Rochelle garland us with frangipani and orchids. No point in resisting being a tourist, for here, unlike in Trinidad, we *are* tourists, visitors on a week's trip, just relieved to be met and chaperoned.

As we drive into Colombo Lawrence says, 'Doesn't it remind you of the Eastern Main Road? San Juan? Tunapuna? The Croissé?' I notice the hoardings and signs. The galvanise houses, the shopfronts and the balconies over the street are all so familiar. Of course we notice the differences too, like the life-sized pictures of the president and the large photographs of the newly appointed Catholic cardinal. Here Buddha sits on every corner. The familiarity yet strangeness is slightly disconcerting. Athula suddenly slams on the breaks. I'm fully awake now. We are at a road check and a soldier carrying a gun looks into the car, unfriendly, unsmiling. The civil war is only recently over and cruelties from both sides are raw in everyone's mind. 'All for the good,' Athula explains. 'Mr President doing his best for everyone.' We glance at each other. In London, the morning we had left, we had heard on the news driving to the airport of the huge demonstration against the Sri Lankan president's visit to London. He is a man accused of crimes against humanity.

The Galle Face Hotel is lit up with a huge Happy Christmas and a Santa Claus skiing across a snowed landscape. We hear the crashing of the sea below us at the end of the promontory. The last guests of a wedding party are leaving as we check in. The musicians are loading huge tassa drums on to a van. At the reception there is a lot of discussion about our booking which we cannot understand. English has given away to Sinhala. Athula assures us that everything will be fine and, as he leaves, he gives us his card – 'Just in case': *Athula Gunawardena Tour Operator.* Finally, we reach our room, still garlanded, but sleepy and dishevelled after our night's journey. It's almost twenty-four hours since we have slept.

The room is enormous and freezing cold, chilled by loud and ancient air conditioners, a stark difference to the tropical night. Although there are baskets of fruit and vases of flowers, this old colonial-style room, with a bed the size of a swimming pool, seems very uninviting. I long for modern comfort. Too tired to complain, we just switch off the air conditioning and crawl under the sheets. I lie there with no sleep coming despite intense fatigue. I can hear Matt's tone of surprise in the Real Holidays office: 'Are you sure you want to stay in the colonial wing? The modern wing has wonderful rooms.' What is it that makes me want to go back in time? Why imagine that the original part of an old hotel that stands close to the old port and harbour where the SS *Oronsay* docked will lead me to Jack and Trudie?

We have a day to recover from our night of travel and to get a glimpse of Colombo thanks to the novelist

Romesh Gunesekera, our Sri Lankan friend from London, who is here to visit the newly opened north of the country and write about what he discovers. We take a short tour of the city and see some of the major sites, as well as the area where Romesh lived as a child.

We sample local delicacies: hoppers, which are bowl-shaped pancakes, and lamprais, savoury delicacies baked in banana leaves. We learn from Romesh more about the complexities of the political situation here. In just a week we will hardly touch the surface of this place. We know, from our visitors' experiences in Trinidad, how hard it is to pick up the subtleties of a country in a short time. We have so often tried to explain Trinidad's social and political mores and just left our friends confused. Now it's our turn to be confused and to be the visitors. We won't be able to go into the northern territory, the old Tamil stronghold, unlike Romesh, who has a special permit. However, we will get as far north as the ancient city of Anuradhapura, which became a capital in 380 BC. It has only recently been reopened to tourists.

I show Romesh the Ceylon extracts from my parents' letters and he points out exactly where the old harbour still stands, where the ocean liners once arrived. Here, when the SS *Oronsay* docked, according to Jack: *natives came on board to do our washing 4d an article and my pair of white shorts came up the whitest they've ever been.*

The travellers on the *Oronsay* had one day only in Ceylon, nineteen hours to be precise. They went to Kandy and back, travelling in an open-sided car on twisting roads – quite a journey! We have chosen to go by train to Kandy in the observation car. Athula has arranged to take us to the station and meet us at the Queen's Hotel in Kandy at lunchtime.

The first-class observation car is hardly as we had imagined it: 'Racatang,' Lawrence announces, using a Trinidad expression. However, I'm very relieved to see there is a toilet. A family of excited Sri Lankan children travelling with their grandparents are waving and calling to their parents as the train pulls off. We pass through the slums of Colombo, the backs of houses and industrial buildings, and we are soon out of the city, bumping down the track. I laugh when I see a monkey running along the top of a passing train. There are so many people at the stations, on the roads and even on the railway line after the train has passed: children in their neat school uniforms, men in sarongs, women in saris. Lawrence is seeing the reminders of his home: East Indian people, rice fields on the plains, egrets, savannahs, Trinidad.

I remember my thrill at seeing the tropics for the first time – Trinidad, 1975. Lawrence was already there visiting his parents, carefully preparing the ground for the arrival of the 'new girlfriend'. I travelled on my own, excited to be flying BWIA, eager to embrace everything West Indian: my Guyanese travelling companion, the beautifully attired air hostesses, the spicy food, the sing-song voices that reminded me a little of Welsh and more of the West Indian students I had taught at Ladbroke Grove. I was leaving sadness behind, the death of my father, and I didn't want to think about my life In England. I was embracing newness, excitement and change.

I arrived in a ramshackle little airport, so different

from the large modern airport at Piarco today. Lawrence helped me fish my bag out of a dump on the ground. His elderly parents were there; they seemed old-fashioned, polite and distant. We drove out into a landscape that took me totally by surprise. I had never imagined colours could be so brilliant. Had I thought the tropics were just a slightly exaggerated form of the Mediterranean? We drove along the Chin Chin Road, the back way to Chaguanas, passing the little wooden houses on stilts with their flowering gardens, brightly dressed people, some in traditional Indian clothes, others in African head-ties, out and about, walking the road, sitting on steps on verandas, on balconies, everywhere. Lawrence was amused and his parents bemused by my enthusiasm. This was just 'the back way home'. The tall palms along the road, 'Palmiste' I learned later, seemed amazing, I hadn't imagined trees so tall. It was dusk when we arrived at the bungalow on the plain. The mountains, dramatic on the horizon, seemed full of mystery. The sounds of the frogs and insects were overwhelming, and in the distance I could hear the tassa drums coming from the Indian village – 'probably a wedding', Lawrence had explained.

After rum punch on the veranda we went into the living room and I moved over to view the pictures on the wall, expecting the etchings to be local scenes, beaches and palm trees. I found myself staring at the one place in the world that I didn't want to see at all. The six etchings were of Shrewsbury, my home town. There were the Shrewsbury School grounds, with the tall oak on the cricket pitch. I had walked through the grounds every day to school, hand in hand with my mother. Next was the Shrewsbury School Hall, Allington Hall, where I had been an angel in the nativity play, all dressed up in gold, my first venture into amateur dramatics. There was the boathouse, with its upper room. I would go to dances there as a teenager. Then there was the Old School Building, which had become the town library, and, finally, a view of the chapel. I could see that spire from my kindergarten window at Stepping Stones.

I look now through the train window and see that we are beginning to climb. Lawrence is staring out at the view.

'Remember how enchanted I was by my first view of the tropics along the Chin Chin Road? And how I discovered Shrewsbury in your living room? Your father's old school.'

'Strange! I was thinking about my father too,' Lawrence replies. 'This journey into the hills is like the foothills of the Central Range, like Brasso Pedro, where my parents lived on a cocoa estate when they were first married. The houses here remind me of the tapia houses of my childhood. It could be home but for the names: Gampaha, Ragama and Polgahawela. They don't sound at all like Brasso Pedro, Gran Couva and Monserrat! No French and Spanish here, or even British, the names are all Sinhala.'

All the time I've known him, Lawrence has enjoyed retrieving his past. It's there in his writing, with both his novels and his poetry. It's there on every wall and shelf of his study. But I was different. I had spent my younger life determined to move on. I needed to forget the place and the people that I loved so I could be normal and happy. Now, years later, I'm doing my damnedest to remember! And it's hard to pull things out of my memory. It's time to return to what I do have: the letters, real and solid in my hands. Yet not that solid. I reach for the page of frail paper with my father's peculiar handwriting describing his journey into the hills of Ceylon en route to Kandy. I empathise with his enthusiasm, his thrill at his first journey in a tropical landscape:

The vegetation was quite the tropical island dream: coconut palms in profusion everywhere – mangoes, breadfruit, paw-paw, bananas, pineapples, cinnamon all growing in abundance and the young green rice was lovely, brilliant green it was.

When I returned home after my first trip to Trinidad I felt bereft. Not at leaving the beauty of the tropical island but at returning home to no home. And I had no Dad to tell about my adventures, to compare notes with about our first experiences of the tropics. Although it was three months since his death, I felt as bereaved as I did the day after. Now I'm enjoying his letters and I wonder why I never asked him more about this trip when I was young. I guess I was so self-absorbed and busy leading my own youthful life that my interest in his past was fairly minimal. I find his letters home to his parents intriguing if at times too selective, too brief, and a little mannered. I study every word for hidden meanings but rarely does he reveal what he is feeling. I read aloud to Lawrence:

It was 72 miles up to Kandy. What struck me particularly

was the flow of life the whole way along the road. People coming and going: some in European dress, some in white vests, some naked except for a loin cloth, others in sarongs, some with turbans on their heads, some bare-headed; there were Buddhist priests in flame coloured sarongs: occasional elephants plodding along the road; and all the time there was a wonderful spring fragrance in the air, incredibly powerful and exciting to the senses.

The train climbs into the hills and we begin to see a different landscape, tea plantations, fruit groves, rubber trees, spice groves. Tall peaks are appearing and deep valleys. I check our journey on my map. We must be passing Adam's Peak and Bible Rock. Trudie's description echoes our view:

The road began to climb and we got into the hill country amongst the tea and rubber plantations, mile after mile they stretched on either side of us. Away on our right was a big flat-topped crag – the Bible Rock – and ahead another steep peak once the den of a band of outlaws 'like your Robin Hood' said our guide. Up and up we climbed passed tree clad gullies, round steep hair-pin bends till at last we topped the hill and went sailing down into a delightful valley with a broad river in which children were bathing and were thoroughly enjoying giving each other showers.

At Kandy station we emerge from our hypnotic journey into the bustle of city life. It is certainly a privilege not to be carrying our luggage. It takes a while to find our way to the Queen's Hotel, a precarious walk through the crowds, the cars and the tuk-tuks. We ask

Queen's Hotel, 2010

directions three times. People are friendly and helpful, though they find our accents difficult to understand. In the end we go into a bakery, where the owner gives exact directions. Eventually we reach the hotel and outside on the street is a worried Athula, convinced that he has lost his two British tourists.

In the imposing entrance hall with its grand staircase and polished mahogany furniture I see that group of British teachers arriving. It's 9 January 1938: *There were five of us in the party to Kandy where we had lunch at the Queen's hotel.* Little Trudie, just four foot and eleven inches, is looking up to Jack, as he explains the importance of eating hot spicy food in a hot climate. As we move into the open dining room, with its old-fashioned long tables, the colonial easy chairs, Morris-style, on the veranda. I hear their voices, my father, my mother:

We lunched at the Queen's Hotel where we indulged in the great variety of curries. I realised that I had never tasted curry before.

We had a wonderful desert; tropical fruits; papaws, mangoes, green tangerines and the most delicious banana imaginable.

Jack and Trudie are here: the old photographs of the hotel in 1938 and the display of china from that period, elegant tea sets and dinnerware, the rooms themselves, the terraces, the gardens. The hotel has not been modernised, it is a relic of that past, and though modern Sri Lanka throngs outside, this place has hardly changed. It is still Ceylon. The group are in the dining room, *Bridget, Margaret, myself, Holmes, Jack, and Dick (Jack's young cabin mate).* Is Trudie sitting next to Jack? Does she still think of him as 'Brother Green' or is he now just Jack? How special has he come to be to her on that journey between Toulon and Ceylon? And what does Jack feel? Attracted? Flattered? Or is he still remembering the unobtainable Joyce?

After our light lunch we follow in their footsteps to the Buddhist temple of the Holy Tooth overlooking the lake. It must have seemed so strange to Trudie, so exotic. What a long way from her mill-town home in Yorkshire. She was not widely travelled before she set off on this trip. The monks in their saffron robes, the pilgrims, the vendors all crowding round the holy places. The constant taking on and off of shoes. But the security checks would not have been there in Trudie's time. We don't follow her on her shopping expedition where she bought a *brooch in the form of a fish made in ivory set in gold with a bright blue stone for an eye* for five shillings.

I remember the fish brooch kept in a tiny inside drawer of her jewel box. She had very little jewellery despite the fact that her grandfather was a jeweller. I can remember every piece she owned. I loved exploring the box: to take out the little gold ring with a pearl from its satin-lined nest, to run my fingers along the bright jade necklace, to open the blue box with the pearl necklace that was promised to me 'when you are older'. Few pieces have survived time and thieves and unexplained disappearances!

We rejoin their footsteps in the botanical gardens on the edge of Kandy. Trudie was thrilled to see the trees and spices growing and amazed at their variety. There were cinnamon, cloves, bay rum, all spice, citronella, balsam, quinine, camphor and patchouli. She was touched that one of the guides climbed the nutmeg tree to find her the fruit. Most of all she loved the orchids: *exquisite, I was given a little bouquet*. It rains while we are there, a light tropical rain that heightens the smells. It must have seemed so foreign to Trudie, so different from Greenhead Park in Huddersfield. Lawrence takes a picture of me under my big umbrella in the spice gardens, walking Trudie's walk and enjoying the pungent aromas that the rain brings. I feel for a moment that I've slipped back in time and almost expect to see the group of English exchange teachers coming round the corner.

'God, look at the time!'

Lawrence's voice brings me back to reality. We realise that we've forgotten all about Athula, who we find waiting for us patiently at the main gate.

'Now I shall take you to a nice tea place, a good hotel not far away,' he informs us.

'But we'd like to go to the Government Rest House,' I say, pointing across the road.

'Not very nice,' he replies curtly.

How to explain that I'm doing a ludicrous thing. I want to go because my mother and father may have had tea there seventy-odd years ago. Before I have to insist he quickly agrees, with a bemused but also amused expression, to leave us there and pick us up later. We feel a bit guilty as he is probably losing a commission and so far we've not been near a gift shop or an obvious tourist attraction.

We have an excellent brew of tea with sandwiches and cake. We love it; the old wooden chairs, the colonial-style sofas, the veranda full of plants, the government workers and civil servants, old men discussing life and politics.

There's more tea to drink at the small tea plantation we visit. First, though, we are shown the plants, the picking and the drying and sorting process. The fields are beautiful, but we have learned enough of the history to know about the ugliness beneath, the colonial history of exploitation. Compulsory pensions and funeral payments still erode the low wages of the Tamil workers. Tea picking is a back-breaking job. I wonder what my parents thought when they visited a small plantation on their way to Kandy. In those days the conditions must have been appalling. Trudie comments: *the tea picker's houses were poor looking affairs, just shelters built of dried mud and thatched with plaited coconut fronds, but most had verandas and a profusion of flowers.*

We learn the complexities of the types and grades of tea from a beautifully dressed young woman who looks as if she's stepped straight out of a brochure advertising Sri Lanka. 'Try as many flavours as you like,' she offers. I decide I like the traditional regular tea best – the one that reminds me of tea at home, long ago.

We reach the Villa Rosa guest house in Dodanwala Passage by winding up and up the small roads above Asgiriya, just north of Kandy. It is perched on a hill with views of the Mahaweli River. After our hectic day we relax on the little veranda. It's straight off our room, which is at the very top of the house. 'Adam's Peak' is what the young guest attendants call it, as they have to run up and down the stairs. Suddenly it's twilight and the hills are lit up, their shapes sharpening. The tall mountains behind us are still covered in cloud, but above the river the sky is clearing. It's time to switch on the lights. Lawrence is scribbling away in his notebook and I am rereading the letters. I imagine Jack and Trudie's journey back from Kandy to the SS *Oronsay* while we watch the sun setting over the brown Mahaweli.

*

Trudie felt exhausted as they left Kandy at half past three. The roads were crowded with traffic: private cars, vans and lorries from the plantations and buffalo carts. Elephants, too, that were being taken down to the river to be washed. She marvelled at how much they had seen and done on this extraordinary day. She began to drift into sleep, although she didn't want to miss a thing.

She woke suddenly as Bridget cried, 'Snake, snake.' A huge snake slid across the road and the car ran right over it. They all turned, expecting to see it squashed flat, but it had survived and glided off into the long grass.

'I wouldn't want to meet that on my pillow,' shuddered Margaret.

'There are ninety-eight species of snakes in Ceylon,' Holmes explained, 'the hooded cobra being the most dangerous.'

Jack's eyes caught Trudie's and he smiled at her as he said, 'No, we wouldn't want to be charmed by that snake.'

They drove at speed down the mountains as the sun was beginning to sink. The light of the late afternoon sharpened every line, lit up every tree. Trudie felt herself tingling with a strange excitement. She felt drunk on beauty, on the sensuous landscape, and yes, she had to admit it, from that smile of recognition she had had from Jack. A smile that seemed to say 'two minds can think the same'.

At Kajugama they stopped for tea at the Government Rest House. The group settled at a table right at the edge of the veranda looking over a small plantation of cashew trees and palms set amid the forest, above a little river, framed by the mountains. Trudie found herself next to Jack on the two-seated Morris-style couch. His arm rested lightly on her shoulder, casually thrown across the back of the seat. He was a tall man. She wondered if this was just for comfort, or was it an indication of something more? They had danced together often enough on board, but he had never, as yet, shown any romantic interest. Today everything felt different.

The waiters arrived with generous pots of tea, slices of thinly cut bread and butter and a plate of perfectly ripened bananas. The group fell silent as they ate their tea and watched the sun set behind the mountains. For a while there seemed to be no breath of air, apart from their own breathing; even the forest seemed still. Then when it was almost dark the palm fronds trembled, the trees swayed and the frogs began to croak and cry, making a noise, Trudie thought, rather like cicadas. From brilliant daylight to dark night had taken the half-hour of their tea. As they clambered into the open car, Trudie chose deliberately, but she hoped not obviously, to sit next to Jack. It was a romantic journey back through the tropical night: the enchanting scents that wafted into the car, the strange and unaccountable noises from the darkness, the occasional sound of drums and Jack so close to her. She had no idea if he felt as she did.

Back on the SS *Oronsay*, too late for dinner, the group had a picnic supper of biscuits and raisins that Trudie found for them. They were from that welcome supply Susie had given her at the beginning of the voyage. Jack suggested they take a turn round the ship and get a last look at Colombo before they sailed. The others declined but she joined him eagerly. He pointed out the landmarks as they leaned together over the deck rail.

'Look over there. You can see the governor's residence all lit up, right there behind the lighthouse. Beyond is Kollupitiya, and Galle Face Green in front of the famous Galle Face Hotel.'

Trudie imagined for a moment fleeing the boat with Jack, leaving all responsibilities behind, spending the night with him in this famous hotel.

'What are you thinking about?' he asked.

'You,' she replied simply. She felt him edge away slightly, then turn and look down at her.

'Don't think about me,' he said gently. 'There are things I've left behind. Just enjoy the beauty of this moment.'

His voice was tender but he made no move towards her. They stayed like that for a while, just side by side, looking towards the city, and then together they turned towards the lights of the ship. He walked her to her cabin and kissed her lightly on her forehead. She whispered, 'Goodnight.'

Lying in her bunk, with Margaret gently snoring, she played the whole day back. Yes! It was her best day ever. And Jack? She was surprised at her own desire, clearly much stronger than his, yet strangely she didn't feel rejected. She knew, instinctively, that she would have to wait; she was just happy to recognise that, after all these years, she had found a man she could love.

*

Love. It's such a simple thing to acknowledge when you are older. It's easy for us. But to know it when you are young is surely impossible. Desire is different. It overcomes the young with such an intensity that, yes, maybe Trudie would have left the *Oronsay* if Jack had desired her. Would she have risked all for a night of passion in the Galle Face Hotel, above the churning of the Indian Ocean?

We are sitting at the end of the main veranda at the

table the waiters call 'World's End', dissecting our day, mulling over each sight and each discovery. We've done and seen so much since we left the Galle Face at six o'clock this morning. It's hard to believe it's just been a day. We are high above the River Mahalewi, almost suspended. Our delightful meal is served by the exquisite Triton. We have named him so after his likeness to the main character in Romesh Gunesekera's *Reef* who prepares and serves food with a similar dedication. I remember Jack's words and I too wonder if I've ever eaten such good curry. We've cheated slightly as we've asked for it 'mild'.

I find the last paragraph of Trudie's letter and read it to Lawrence:

So much for Ceylon, our last port of call before Fremantle. Before starting the voyage I had always thought of the day Daddy and I got lost on the moors in Scotland as the best day of my life but after our wonderful day in Toulon I considered I'd had two 'best days' and now of course there are three.

Like Trudie, this has been a very special day for us, but *the best day?* It's impossible to judge, too many to remember them all, after so many years together. The next morning, over breakfast with a steaming pot of the best local tea, Lawrence hands me the poem he has written: 'At the Villa Rosa'. It ends:

Car horns, tuk-tuks, the blow of the train, or a lorry
The ordinary world rattles along under the Buddha's gaze
As we continue our pilgrimage.

CHAPTER 3 – Into the Forest

THE SMALL GREEN ADDRESS BOOK measures approximately three inches by two and it is only half an inch thick at the most, and yet in it is all that's left of my mother's world. I found it at the bottom of an old tin of assorted family photographs. Somehow, it had survived the years, avoiding getting thrown away in the huge clear-out of our old house in Shrewsbury. Somehow, it missed being misplaced.

The title page is clear:

G P Landsborough
94 Fitzwilliam Street
Huddersfield. 1940.

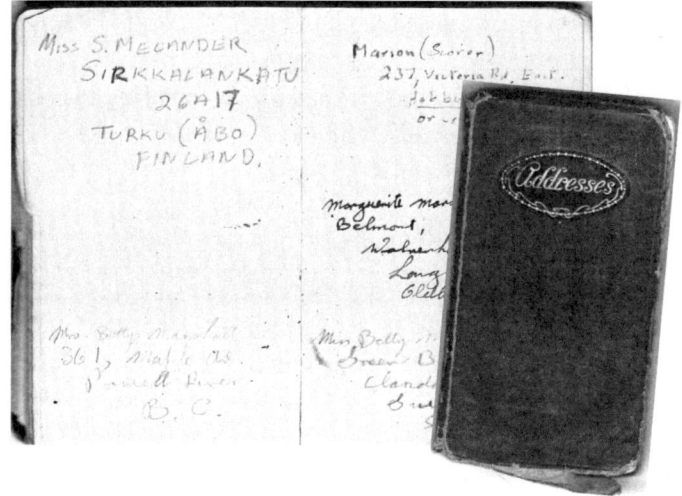

The early pages have suffered from damp. I can just make out Bridget's and Hilda's names but not the addresses. The later pages tell their stories, yield her family, friends and acquaintances. This is where I discovered, shortly before we left for our trip, that Sandy and Miss Sandilands were one and the same, that Mrs Woolcock ran the boarding house at 17 Avonmore Road, Cottesloe, and that Uncle John and family lived at 4 Vaucluse Street, Claremont, until they moved to Ord Street in 1940. She must have corresponded with some of her Australian friends, Mrs Greatorex, Miss Ryan and Hilda Burnside, after she returned to England. My father's London addresses look carefully recorded, in clear capitals under the Gs: Mr J Green, 78 Underhill Rd, Dulwich, SE22, then a tiny arrow points across to the next page and 45 Crestway, Roehampton. I never knew my father lived there.

I treasure this address book. There is so little in the archive, so little to retrieve: my memories of her stories; the boomerang, which is the only remaining memento of those 'treasures' she brought back from Australia and kept in the cabinet in the attic; a few photographs; and, most importantly, the wonderful set of letters to her family.

'When I lived in Australia...', 'When I went round the world...', 'When I very first met your daddy...' Yes, I remember those openings, but little of what followed. I knew everything was 'upside down', like the black swans on the white lakes. I loved to hear, as small children do, all about the animals, the koalas and the wallabies, the kangaroos and the kookaburras, the emus and the flying foxes. I longed to see them too. The stuffed duck-billed platypus was my favourite and I played with him until his bill fell off and had to be mended with Sellotape. I longed to throw the boomerang that was kept on the top shelf of the cabinet, out of reach of childish hands. Most of all, I loved the shiny pile of wooden blocks, 'all from different gum trees', my mother explained. I had no idea what a gum tree was but imagined it was something to do with the gum that I wasn't allowed to chew.

I remember someone called Hilda coming to stay when I was about eight. I realise now it must have been Hilda Burnside. There was a lot of talk about Australia, and my brother and I had to sit quietly and listen. Then the transparencies came out of their yellow box in the stationery drawer. We looked at them through a bigger box with a light at the end. I found it quite difficult at first to see them. I remember pictures of wallabies and koalas, and shots of strange vegetation and a bungalow with a veranda which wasn't like the veranda at my friend's Noreen's house across the road. And people that I didn't know.

The loss of this box of slides, or 'transparencies' as my mother called them, still annoys and puzzles me. I had them, I'm sure, when Lawrence and I first bought the house in Trinder Road in 1975. For a time they were in the drawer in the mahogany table in our bedroom, I remember quite distinctly, but somewhere in our life of coming and going to Trinidad they must have got thrown out. All but two. They, sadly, are of the bush not the people.

*

Our arrival in Perth on 11 December 2010 isn't quite as simple as we expect. Changing at Singapore after our two-hour night flight from Sri Lanka was 'easy-peasy' as Matt, back in Real Holidays, had assured us it would be. We even had time for breakfast, as the airport was so efficient. We helped ourselves with delight to the red glossy apples on offer from large bowls in Departures. Now at Customs in Perth we are sniffed out by dogs. I can't think why we are being led to one side until our apples are extracted.

'Look! It's written here quite clearly, "No fruit or cereals or foodstuff of any kinds to be brought into the country. No boots with soil on them,"' barks the Customs officer. 'What about *your* boots?'

'I haven't got any boots with me,' Lawrence lies nonchalantly, and I visualise the red mud from Anuradhapura that is stuck in the crevices of his walking boots. I feel nervy and apprehensive. I'm half expecting to be barred from entry.

Eventually we are through Customs and free, here in Australia, where I've been dreaming of coming since I was a child. As we travel by taxi into the city I wonder what I will discover of my mother's life here all these years on. Looking through the taxi window, on first appearance Perth seems a totally modern city with a small centre of skyscrapers and a large urban sprawl.

We stay the first two nights in a 'short stay' holiday apartment, Riverview, on Mount Street, near the botanical gardens that overlook the Swan River. We can easily walk into the centre and find the little bits of 'old Perth' that still remain: the cricket ground where Trudie saw Don Bradman play for Western Australia – *the*

Australian fielding was superb – and the old theatre where she saw *the Marcus show, a magnificently picturesque variety show, hot from New York; most glorious frocks (when there were any) beautiful stage settings and perfect figures.*

The once-thriving city centre, where the old buildings remain, is now downtown grot, away from the bustle of the rich business quarter. It's on Hay Street where Trudie went window-shopping, looking at the new short hemlines of the skirts and deciding to shorten hers. *They're up to the knees here,* she wrote to Susie; *are they being worn shorter at home?* The Carlton Hotel, at the east end of Hay Street, next to the Backpackers, is where Auntie and Uncle would take Trudie for a treat. It is run-down. What was once elegant is now seriously shabby. There's a large hand-painted sign outside advertising 'Bucks and Hens Nights, Birthdays, and Anything You Want'. The bartender is amused at our request to look around. 'You won't find nothing here of interest,' he laughs, 'but help yerselves.' We do find mementoes of the past in the upstairs rooms, which are now used for storage. A grand piano is pushed into a corner, a few old oil paintings are still hanging. We discover some interesting photographs of this street in the 1940s that give an idea of the elegance of the old city.

Yet I'm nowhere nearer to finding Trudie. I search through the tattered phone directory in our apartment looking for a Richard or an Isabel Pearce, Trudie's young cousins. According to my family tree, Isabel would be eighty-two now and Dick eighty-six. Was Isabel married? Would she still be a Pearce? There are so many Pearces in the book, I can't possibly ring them all. Should I try ancestory.co.uk? Having no precise dates of birth on the family tree and no addresses, I doubt I would discover anything. And would it be an intrusion if I did find them? I stare at the lists, focusing on the R. Pearces. I imagine my queries: 'Are you Richard Pearce? Do you remember your cousin Gertrude, who stayed with you in 1938?' He probably would just say no and put down the phone.

*

On our last afternoon at Riverview, before we leave for the bush, we meet up with Lawrence's cousin Esmond and his wife, Frances Anne. Lawrence has been quite nervous about the meeting as he's not seen his cousin for nearly fifty years. They were very close friends as children but have not kept in touch as adults. Their lives have diverged. Esmond has lived away from Trinidad most of his life and, after work in the oil business, he has become a high-powered business and management consultant here in Perth. We wait rather anxiously for them in the little foyer, wondering how it will all pan out.

Esmond is still doing business on the phone as they drive us round the city, but Frances Anne is eager to discover all about my 'family project'. She's thrilled at the idea of tracking down places and maybe even people. Lawrence is keen too and before I have a chance to object he gives them Trudie's first address, at Vaucluse Street in Claremont. I had planned to go there on our drive out of Perth tomorrow.

I feel peculiar as we turn into the street whose name I've seen so often at the top of Trudie's letters. As we arrive at number 4, I recognise the veranda running all around the house, just like in the slide of long ago, the leafy garden, the white wooden one-storey house.

'Don't you want to take some photographs?' asks Frances Anne eagerly.

How to explain? I just want to drive away as quickly as possible. Not only does this visit seem pointless but now the whole expedition seems ludicrous. I get out of the car obediently and self-consciously take some shots. I hope no one in the house is watching.

'Shall I go up and see if there's anyone there?' Lawrence suggests.

'Yes,' Frances Anne agrees. 'They might know the history of the house.'

'No,' I say quickly, and I'm relieved to find the quiet Esmond coming to my support. He suggests we drive on to look at Fremantle.

I don't want to go to Fremantle either. I want to see it tomorrow, alone with Lawrence and the letters, but how to say this without sounding rude and ungrateful? I stay quiet.

We end up in a bar in Cottesloe, probably a stone's throw from Trudie's digs on Avonmore Road. This time, to my relief, Lawrence says nothing. Everyone relaxes now. Esmond has finished with his work. I'm happy to be away from my family history and we turn comfortably to talk of Trinidad and all the relatives in this enormous family of Langes and Scotts, catching up on brothers and sisters, cousins and aunts, and the hundreds of nephews and nieces, great-nephews and nieces, and now even great-great-nephews and nieces. Esmond and Frances Anne have just one daughter, who was adopted, and one very precious granddaughter, and we have none, so we all understand what it's like to be a small unit in an enormous crowd. Lawrence and Esmond are now happily back into recognisably Trinidad lingo as memories of childhood resurface.

'Why were you so cross at first?' Lawrence asks when we get back to Riverview.

'I'm sorry. I know this meeting was important for you. But I just didn't want to share my dead family with your living one.'

He hugs me despite my harsh reply and fetches the photocopied letters, then reads aloud parts of the first letter that Trudie sent from Vaucluse Street:

Dearest Mother, Dads, and All,
I'm sitting in the shade of the verandah to write this, there is a gentle breeze blowing, it is gloriously warm and it seems impossible that just over a month since I was shivering in Tilbury. It was in the middle of breakfast that we tied up so I wasn't there to look for Auntie Alice. However Uncle John, Isabel, and Richard came on the boat and I was walking straight past them when Uncle said 'excuse me but I wonder if you know Miss Landsborough'. I recognized him then of course... a Pearce, though shorter than either Uncle Ernest or Uncle Charlton. Then Auntie arrived and I showed them around the boat and said goodbye to my large group of friends. It seems so sad that we make such good friends for so short a while and then we have to say good-bye. Perhaps I'll see some of them on the

return. Bridget and Jack (Brother Green) and I talked of crossing the States together, but that's a long time ahead yet.

'She's clearly quite sad to be saying goodbye to Jack,' Lawrence suggests, 'and hoping to meet him again.'

'Her feelings must've been quite mixed at this point, excitement at arriving but sorry the boat trip has ended.'

Lawrence flicks to the last page:

Here at Vaucluse street we have spent the day talking. I have given them all the news from home and shown Isabel the photograph of Henry. She was clearly very impressed with him when he visited here with Mother! I think both Isabel and Dick are lovely young people. I hope all young Aussies are like them then I shall really enjoy my year's work here. Hope all of you are well at home the family send their love and special remembrances to Henry.

'Of course,' says Lawrence, 'what you discuss with your family or write to your family is only the partial truth, the spin so to speak. I know it well!'

'But thank goodness for letters,' I say, as I put this one back in its place among the rest of the photocopies. 'Even if partially a spin, at least we can read between the lines. For future generations no lines at all.' And then I add, 'But for us no future generation.'

4 Vauclose Street

*

The next morning we set off on our trip south to the bush and the coast. First we return to Cottesloe, where we find the location of 17 Avonmore Road. This is where Mrs Woolcock rented out a room and gave Trudie her weekday meals for twenty-five shillings. Sadly, number 17 has gone... and quite recently too, it seems, as the other old houses on the street are still there. There's just a gap now with a fig tree and the view of the sea. Soon there'll be a new house.

The big ships are still passing by, carrying not post or passengers but cargo from all over the world.

*

It was Trudie's first night at her new digs in Cottesloe. Her bedroom was sorted thanks to the help of her new friend, Miss Sandilands, who was also on exchange and had come out on an earlier boat. Mrs Woolcock had said that if the little bedroom at the back of the house on the main road got too warm, then Trudie was welcome to sleep out on the veranda at the front, facing the sea and getting the breeze. She was finding the room unbearably hot, so she quietly moved through the house to the veranda and lay out on the divan. It was pitch black as the clouds covered the stars.

There was a cooling breeze. She dozed.

She woke suddenly to a loud rumble of thunder. The sky lit up and the rain came in huge splashes. She had never seen rain like it. The lightning flashed in zigzags, like storybook pictures of tempests, and, almost at once, the thunder cracked, suggesting the eye of the storm was right overhead. The rain was now splashing on to the veranda. Trudie decided to retreat. The thunderclaps were frightening, as loud as exploding bombs. This was what she'd heard about – electric storms.

Back in the little bedroom there was no way she could sleep. She picked up her novel, *Persuasion*, and tried to find her way back into the life of Anne Elliot. Suddenly she was in total darkness. The lights had blown. She heard noises coming from the rest of the house and cautiously made her way to the living room, where Mrs Woolcock and her children were lighting candles.

'Welcome to life down under,' said Mrs Woolcock, smiling. 'Perth is the place of heat and storms, especially in summer.'

They played rummy first, then Trudie introduced

them to Lexicon. She looked forward to telling Susie, when she next wrote, how useful this little card game had been on a number of occasions.

When she finally got to bed her mind was racing and sleep seemed impossible. She let her thoughts return to her most precious memories, the best way she always found to drift off. She imagined herself and Dads walking on the moors at Crocketford, up at Johnny Turner's, where you can see as far as Criffel and the Solway Firth. Dads would tell her of his boyhood up here, 'a hard and healthy life, lassie – aye, it were a good job I was such a grand fisherman, kept the family fed on the best food in God's world. I wish I could sew coats like I catch fish!' Then there was Celyon: the journey back from Kandy, sunlight turning so quickly into dusk, sitting on the veranda of the Government Rest House with Jack next to her, his arm gently resting on her shoulder.

The next day was hot, lazy weather, not a cloud in sight, the kind of heat that made Trudie want to do nothing but lie out and hope for a breeze. It was baking inside the house. Mrs Woolcock and the children were all in the living room, so Trudie and Miss Sandilands escaped into the garden. They dragged out the blankets from Trudie's bed and lay on them under the fig tree, skirts pulled up, sleeves rolled back, stockings rolled down and shoes kicked off.

'Are you enjoying your new digs?' Miss Sandilands asked.

'Rather a dramatic start with the storm! Yes, I like the Woolcocks and I'm enjoying my independence from Uncle and Auntie. They tend to treat me in the same way as they treat Isabel and Dick. They forget I'm all of twenty-seven! Still, they've been really kind, welcoming me as one of the family and showing me Perth. It was good to begin the year there.'

'Aye, you were lucky to have relations to settle you in. But you've found a good place here and such a view!'

They both looked up. Beyond the garden they had a clear sight of the sea. They looked at a ship ploughing along towards Fremantle. Trudie wondered if there were letters from home on board.

'I do get a little homesick,' she admitted.

'Me too,' Miss Sandilands agreed.

As they chatted about the Australian school system and the differences between here and home, they slipped into the informal address of 'Sandy' and 'Trudie'. They agreed that the children were lovely to teach.

'Much easier than those Glaswegian hooligans that I teach at home!' Sandy said.

'They really enjoy hearing about Britain. They ask me things about the royal family that I have no idea about!'

They agreed that the social life in Perth and its suburbs was too constrained, too formal.

'Not a suitable man in sight,' moaned Sandy, 'at least not to meet. You have to go to cricket and enjoy them from afar!'

Trudie described the invitations she had received to bridge parties, tea, Monopoly parties and church. 'Yes,' she sighed, 'the life of the schoolmistress.'

Later, as they lay back on the blankets looking up at the southern stars, Trudie's thoughts drifted back to the

Oronsay. She hadn't felt homesick on the whole journey out. There had been so much to do, not just the trips ashore but the life on board: dancing and deck quoits, table tennis competitions, concerts and conversations at dinner about all sorts of things with Jack.

Sandy interrupted her thoughts. 'We should plan to do something exciting,' she suggested. 'Let's take a trip. Let's explore this great country, shake off suburban Perth for a few days over the Easter holidays.'

*

We locate the old harbour in Fremantle, where the *Oronsay* docked and Trudie stepped ashore to her new life. It is overshadowed by the large modern harbour, which is a busy working port. The railway station, where Trudie arrived every day from Cottesloe, remains intact, with its polished fretwork and shining gold roof. The architecture of many of the houses and shops is preserved. So, on first appearance, it must look as Trudie saw it. But it's not a working town in the same way. Fremantle, or 'Freo' as the locals call it, is 'upmarket' and 'arty'. It's where Lawrence's cousin Esmond goes out to eat and Frances Anne does boutique shopping. We have coffee in a trendy bar, Café 55, on a corner that looks down the attractive main street, South Terrace, with its balconied historic buildings now housing Fremantle's famous 'cappuccino strip'.

We take off in the car to look for South Terrace Primary. My research on Google has given me a brief history of the school, so I know what I'm likely to find of Trudie's South Terrace – a bit of brick wall now attached to the modern hospital. After taking photographs of my wall, and of the old houses opposite that once faced the school, we decide to go into the new school across the road from the hospital. It is still called South Terrace and it may have some archives. The receptionist politely explains that it's the end-of-term staff party and she wouldn't want to intrude. She herself knows nothing about the history of the school or old records. 'But you are welcome to look at the photographs from the old school,' she adds as an afterthought, and points to the walls of the entrance hall. We've been standing in front of them, a whole series of black and white photographs of the old school, the grounds, views of the old houses opposite and, finally, the pupils. As I stand and look at the photographs of the pupils, I peer closely to see if any members of staff are sitting among them, like on my old school photographs where they took the front row. But no, it's just the smaller boys with their short trousers and bare legs neatly crossed. I notice the date on one: 1939. This was my mother's time. These could be her pupils! I get that odd feeling in my chest as if I want to weep. It feels like one step closer. So little really, but it helps me imagine the young Trudie *here*. It gives me back a tiny bit of her life.

Her letters are full of her pupils: how much she enjoyed taking them out on trips, particularly to cricket, how the headteacher was impressed with her modern approaches to PE, how tricky it was to teach concepts of the ice age in geography when these children had never seen snow. She described in one letter home their questions about England: *Have you seen the King and*

Queen? Have you been skiing? I had to confess that I'd never seen the little princesses, Jean Batten, Amy Johnson, or the Duke and Duchess of Windsor, though I had been to Switzerland for Winter Sports! In another letter she described an invitation to the home of a pupil: *they were very poor, but scrupulously clean. And so generous in what they offered me. The girl is a delightful lass and, I think, remarkably bright, I hope she will go far and will be given the appropriate scholarships.*

*

From Fremantle we plan to follow Trudie south on that journey into the bush that she and Sandy went on during their four-day Easter holiday in 1938. I have the letters on my lap, with the map and the Lonely Planet, of course. Lawrence drives. I want to find the lake just past the road to Rockingham where, Trudie writes, *we passed a long stretch of water on our right, almost white in colour and on it of course were flocks of black swans. It's surprising how many things here are, to our English eyes, upside down or the wrong way round.*

'I'm not seeing any sign of a lake,' Lawrence interrupts my thoughts.

'It should be right here,' I insist. 'We've just passed the sign to Rockingham.'

'Lakes can dry up, landscapes can change, roads are rebuilt and boundaries are altered.'

I fall silent. I know he's right. I just want to see for myself the lake that my mother had described to me. As if, by magic, it will open my memory to her voice, to her other stories, to her.

On our left the Darling Range is covered with the bright yellow of the Christmas trees. On our right we get occasional glimpses of sand dunes and ocean. The strange-looking stunted balga trees are everywhere, with their grassy tops and flower stalks. 'Black boy' was their name in Trudie's day, denoting that colonial world she belonged to in 1938.

I notice the metal road sign with a kangaroo picture warning motorists to watch out. 'Bet you hardly ever see one of those,' I say, 'unless you are really in the bush.' A few moments later, I see him, hopping along the road. I think for a moment it is a tall man jumping up and down, then I shout, 'Kangaroo!'

We laugh at him. We giggle. He looks so strange and unworldly. He is like all the many pictures we have seen and yet he's different. He's so big. He looks as if he both belongs and yet doesn't. The fast cars shooting by, the tarmac road, the metal posts, these shouldn't be his world.

'He's our good omen,' Lawrence says, 'the lucky charm for our journey.'

*

Sandy had been as good as her word and had immediately booked a coach trip down the south-west coastal and forest areas for the few days they were free over the Easter weekend. They found themselves on a comfortable coach named Miss Yalingup in the two seats right at the front next to the driver. As soon as he and some others of the party realised that there were two young 'pommies' on board, they were given lots of useful information, along with teasing, silly nonsense and leg-pulling:

'Look at that kangaroo hopping along!'

'Where, where?'

'Just joking,' laughed Alick, the driver. ' You British imagine roos on every corner!'

Trudie felt overwhelmed by happiness; the sheer joy of being young and alive, and on the other side of the world. It must be the sunshine, the warm autumn weather, the excitement of leaving the suburbs and the strangeness of the landscape. She had missed that thrill of travelling that she had felt on the journey out, seeing all those places across the world. The last three months had gone slowly. In comparison with life on the *Oronsay* Claremont and Cottesloe had seemed dull. Yes! What was missing was fun. She loved to have fun and adventure and sensed that Sandy did too.

She looked over at the hills of the Darling Range on her left. The flowering trees were changing now.

Autumn was here. The Christmas trees had lost their golden heads. The yellow grass had turned to a deep green.

That first day, after seeing the flocks of black swans at Rockingham, they drove along the coast with sand dunes on their right and glimpses of the sea, through the pretty seaside town of Mandurah, where they had morning tea, and then on to Bunbury for lunch. There they turned inland through orchard country to Donnybrook to spend the first night in a rather old-fashioned hotel. It was a cold night and heating was scarce in the rooms. They stayed up late by the log fire playing Lexicon and feeling too warm and cosy to go up to bed. When they finally settled in for the night and Trudie was dropping off she heard Sandy complain, 'I'm freezing. Wish we could have stayed at the Rose in Bunbury.' She got up to find some socks. 'Now that's what I call a hotel!'

'Yes, it was a most elegant lunch. But we wouldn't have had the right clothes for dinner.'

'We might have met two handsome Australian businessmen who would have swept us off our feet and bought us emeralds and furs!'

'I wish,' laughed Trudie. 'They don't even exist in Perth.'

'Anyone back home?' Sandy asked.

Trudie thought about Cousin Gordon, but nothing had really come of that.

'No, not really,' she admitted.

'Me neither. I was hoping I'd have met a nice Aussie by now!'

'There was someone I liked on the ship,' Trudie

admitted, 'but he hasn't written, as yet. And nothing really happened anyway.' Then, deliberately changing the subject, she said, 'I've been wondering how on earth we'll manage to get a good bath, or even a wash. There's one bathroom for everyone!'

She lay awake for a while, thinking about Jack. She hadn't heard from him and she had expected a letter. It was over two months now. He'd promised to write but she'd not even had a card. It wasn't that she was expecting declarations of love, but she did think that they had become good friends. Susie was probably right about men – better off without them!

Next morning Trudie managed to get only three inches of warm water out of the chip-heater for her bath but at least the open fire that heated the water didn't blow up. She discovered she had caused a long queue for the bathroom as it had taken her so long to work the heater. They were teased on the bus again, this time for not understanding Australian hot-water systems.

*

After our night at the pleasantly old-fashioned Rose Hotel in Bunbury, which Trudie had found 'modernised', we drive south following the coast road, a different route from Trudie's. The shore at Margaret River, famous for surfers, is deserted; schools are not yet 'out' for Christmas, the season has not yet begun. We watch a loan surfer mount the huge ocean waves. We stare out at the sea, conscious of the miles and miles before any land. Somewhere out there is Antarctica. It is the bright light which gives this feeling of vastness, of space. Among the dunes are myriad sweet-smelling wild flowers, yellows, purples, reds. I think of Tim Winton's novel *Breath* as we breathe in the salty air, how he describes the intense pleasure of the surf, his boy hero hooked on riding the great waves.

From there we turn inland into the great forests of the southern outback. On the map there's a small road through the bush which should lead us to Nannup, where we will rejoin Trudie's route. From the bright light we drive into shade, through the karri forest, amazed at the giant trees which reach to such great heights. Are we on the right road? We drive on and on through a tunnel of trees. Not a car passes us; no one is behind or in front.

'We must come to somewhere soon,' I say. 'Some form of habitation where we can check our route.'

'At least we have a full tank.'

We are waiting for the junction to Morven to show up, the way to Rose Glen and on to Nannup, but we find we're on the Rose Brook Road, not the Rose Glen Road. We're lost. Maybe. At last we come across a convenience store. It seems the last stop in the world. An old Aussie, tall, weather-beaten and creased, stands as still as the trees themselves, behind his counter. Does anyone ever stop here? He grunts as we enter. He ignores our questions on junctions and the road to Morven that we think we've missed. He keeps to the main point, our way forward. 'It's Nannup yers want, ain't it?' He knows the road as well as his list of dry goods scribbled in hieroglyphs on the long sheets of brown paper on his counter. He tears off an end and begins to draw a map.

All the time he draws, he drawls, 'Just keep on going, you'll get to Sue's Road. If you can't go straight, the roads been a-mending a while now, then turn right. You'll hit the highway after a time. It'll take you a while. Turn left for Nannup. It's a big country here.' He laughs and looks straight at us, like he knows we're from little Islands. He somehow makes us feel small, this tall man among the tall trees.

It takes us a while to reach the crossroad and the road ahead *is* closed, as the tree-man said. Following his map, we turn right.

Not a car passes us along this lonely road. The trees get bigger and the road gets darker. Then there are great patches of burnt forest which let the light in. The burnt areas are strangely beautiful, the trunks black and the leaves gold. The skeletal shapes are like modern sculptures. We both feel a little unnerved, a touch claustrophobic, in this strange world of silence. I think about how I don't know this land. I have no idea about the hundreds of different kinds of eucalyptus, or gum trees as the locals call them. We are on the very edge of a massive continent.

*

The route Trudie and Sandy were following took them from Donnybrook to Balingup, where the party stopped for morning coffee at the small Balingup inn. Here they branched off the main road on to a corrugated track which felt like driving over a scrubbing board. They drove into a deep valley that followed the Blackwood River. There were huge trees, different kinds of eucalyptus that covered the valley floor, but every so often they caught glimpses of the dark river flowing between the trees and reflecting the foliage overhead. Among the trees flew hundreds of brilliantly coloured parrots all screaming to the same tune.

'They're twenty-eights,' explained Alick. 'Listen carefully. That's what they're calling.'

They listened and heard the rhythm of the birds' call. They repeated together, 'Twenty-eight, twenty-eight,' and the others laughed, enjoying the curiosity and pleasure of the two British visitors. Then the whole bus started singing. They found they knew many of the same old songs: 'Ten green bottles', 'I'll sing you one oh' and 'Ten men went to mow'. As they drew up to the hotel in Nannup for lunch there was a raucous chorus of 'We're here because we're here, because we're here'. Before they got out, Alick told them to look for the infamous Nannup tiger, a rare survivor from prehistoric times.

'Now,' asked Trudie, 'are you pulling my leg or not?'

After the huge lunch at Nannup's surprisingly smart hotel, Sandy and Trudie wandered through the little town with its weatherboard houses. They were amazed at the flowers still blooming in autumn, huge chrysanthemums, daisies of all kinds, jacarandas and agapanthus. They stopped at the stationers to try and buy postcards of this beautiful spot. The shopkeeper, a small wiry man, was delighted. He not only brought out a large array of postcards, but also a huge selection of his own photographs. They were looking for some of the local wildlife.

'Any pictures of the twenty-eights?' asked Trudie.

'I'm not good on birds,' he admitted, 'not got the patience.'

'Well, what about the Nannup tiger, then?' Sandy asked. 'Does it really exist?'

'An old tale,' he said. 'Extinct long ago, I'm sure, though they do say Tasmania still has large cats. But you may well see a quokka. It looks like a large rat – see here.' He held up a picture of a strange-looking little creature. 'It's a marsupial, the same family as kangaroos and wallabies, but very much smaller, more like a possum. I'm Mr de Neve,' he continued, as he took their payment, 'from Switzerland. And where in Great Britain do you ladies hale from?'

'I'm a Yorkshire girl,' Trudie explained, 'and my friend is from Glasgow.'

'Ah, a wee Scottish lass,' replied the little man. 'I miss Europe, but I can never return.'

They looked at him enquiringly, but he didn't explain.

'Look at this,' he said, perhaps wanting to change the subject. He pushed forward a large sheet of cardboard on which was a map of the settlement and photographs of the swimming pool and recreation ground in various stages of development. Foremost among the workers was this Mr de Neve and a note at the bottom read: 'In grateful appreciation of the work done for the youth of Nannup'.

'And have you got children, family, nephews and nieces?' Sandy asked.

'Not here,' he replied curtly. Then he dug out some magazines. 'These are what inspire me.' He showed them artistic photographs from America in the

Illustrated Coronet. There were portraits, landscapes and wild animals. 'I have it delivered every month. It keeps me in touch.'

They heard the bus tooting loudly and realised they were being called.

'We're off to Pemberton now, Mr de Neve. It was lovely to meet you. Good luck with the photography.'

'Lovely to meet you both, too.' Then he added sadly, 'You from the other side.'

*

What a relief when we finally get to Nannup, out of the forest into a small oasis. There are brightly painted weatherboard buildings and cottage gardens full of flowers. There are a mixture of native plants and tropical and temperate shrubs. The purple jacarandas are in flower, and so are the oleanders and the bougainvillea, among the roses and chrysanthemums. I remember a line in my mother's letter: *the chrysanthemums here would rival anything at the Yorkshire show.*

'This would have been exactly the same when Trudie was here!' Lawrence's words echo my thoughts. We soon come to the *high class hotel* where Trudie had enjoyed a good lunch: *but oh what chickens, they'd roasted for us, four or five judging by the number of legs, and served beautifully with three 'veg' and potatoes followed by as many sweets as one could wish, four varieties but repetitions ad lib.*

We stand and look up at the fretwork veranda. A man and woman of about our age smile and ask us where we're from. I hadn't realised it looked so obvious that we are strangers.

'Oh, we just know everyone who lives here,' the woman said.

I ask if the hotel serves lunch.

'Not done lunches in years,' the man replies, 'but there's a nice little café which should be open down by the river. Just carry straight on, you can't miss it.'

So here we sit above the trees on the veranda, ploughing our way through huge portions of vegetable lasagne. Below us, under the trees, is a quokka who is clearly hoping for a titbit, but we have learned not to feed the wild things.

'Have you been to our little museum?' the waitress asks.

We are probably the only tourists who have visited for a while. She directs us just over the road to a tiny building that we haven't noticed. I feel a surge of excitement at the thought of the archival material that I might discover. I turn the door handle, but it is firmly locked.

'We'll find a way,' Lawrence says with his usual optimism when it comes to research. 'There's bound to be an information centre somewhere in a historic village like this.'

We pass a large tourist sign which describes the legendary Nannup tiger. Apparently there have been few sightings in the past hundred years and scientists believe it to be extinct. A few yards further on we see a woman locking up a little information hut. I run across and ask if we can visit the museum.

'Look, have the key,' she says with absolute trust. 'Pop it through the letter box here when you've finished.'

Once inside the museum we are in complete darkness. Eventually, we find the switches hidden under the blinds. As it grows light, we see hundreds of black and white photographs around the walls and on display boards. I read a large sign: 'The History of Nannup'. I soon discover a photograph labelled 'SC 22 Nannup Balingup Road 1936'. It is the very scenic road that Trudie had described along the Blackwood River: *these roads are simply tracks with no surfacing just earth, and with traffic going over them they take on these corrugations running from side to side a foot or two wide.* I can see the huge scrubbing-board humps and the bush growing right into the road.

'Hope it's in better condition now!' I show it to Lawrence. 'This is the next road we're taking.'

A little while later I hear him gasp. 'What have you found?' I ask quickly.

'Mr de Neve. He's right here, and these must be some of his photographs.'

I rush to the other side of the little room. There is the exact picture that Trudie had described. Mr de Neve and three young boys in front of the swimming pool he had built for the young people of Nannup. The label reads: 'SC 114 Ted de Neves Swimming Pool, Nannup'. It has lost its original caption of thanks but the photograph is here! It is difficult in this picture to get a clear view of the *little wiry man* that Trudie had described. However, in the next photograph, 'Mr Teddy de Neve in his garden 1930s', he is absolutely clear. He is small but looks strong and healthy, clearly an outdoors man as well as a committed photographer. I feel as if I've discovered my mother herself! It's as if reading the letters have given me her voice, but actually seeing what she has described so exactly is giving me her.

We photograph the photographs and wonder which of these of 1930s Nannup photographs Mr de Neves had taken himself. There are the newspaper shop and stationers that he ran; there is the hotel, exactly as it is today but with a horse and cart in front, the church, the gardens and the river. Sadly none of the photographs name the photographer.

Outside in the bright light I take a photograph, just a snap on my digital, of the building I now know was Mr de Neve's shop. I shut my eyes and imagine those young women dashing out and clambering back on the bus. I can hear them shouting, 'Wait for us, Alick! Wait for us, everybody!'

*

Trudie and Sandy were amazed as they entered the forest. There were trees reaching up 200 feet on either side of the narrow road and stretching as far as you could see. At first there were the grey, rather smooth trunks of the jarrahs and the thick, rough bloodstained boles of the red gums, interspersed with the short spiky 'black boys'. Every so often they'd meet a region that had been swept by fire, a few bare, gaunt, hollow trunks still standing and many weird animal-shaped burnt-out trunks strewn on the ground, or propping each other up. At last they reached a belt of karri, the real timber. Here the perfectly straight white boles often reached 100 feet before branching. They drove for mile after mile through these great trees. Sometimes they'd see stretches of burnt trees on land cleared for grazing. They seemed stark and gruesome.

'They're like ghost forests.' Trudie whispered to Sandy.

'Don't!' Sandy shuddered. 'I wish we'd arrive in Pemberton. This landscape is beginning to depress me, it's so burned out, so completely lifeless.'

Trudie sank back into her own world. She had been thinking of home again. It was strange this feeling of homesickness that came over her every so often, like a real illness. The chocolate-coloured spaniel at the hotel in Balingup that made her think of Sally had set it off this morning. Now this dark route through the forest reminded her of a journey she'd done as a child with Dads. They had walked through woods together, the Mabie forest it was, near Crocketford. He had shown her how to lay a trail so you could always find your way back home. Home in Crocketford, the croft, the welcome you'd get from Auntie Maggie and Auntie Mina! In her last letter Susie had said that Dads was up there now, having a break from work and doing some fishing.

She was awakened from her reflections by Alick. 'We are now arriving in Pemberton,' he announced. 'It's noted for three things: its saw mills, the swimming pool and the giant karri presented by the governor.'

Trudie and Sandy decided to nip off on their own. They'd had enough of the trees, knew now all about their height and width and which trees were best to make what furniture. So they avoided the big hotel where the rest of the party were having refreshments before the trip to the giant karri. They ambled through the village and discovered two small shops, a haberdashery and a curio shop. They rooted round in both, looking for possible souvenirs of their trip.

'They're not used to tourists, are they?' whispered Sandy in the little odds and ends shop.

Trudie, though, had spotted something she wanted. It was a pile of wood. The pieces were each about ten by five inches and maybe two inches thick. They had been polished. Underneath each was a label: 'Karri', 'Jarrah', 'Red gum'.

'Perfect,' she said. 'I can carry these great trees home in my bag.'

Behind the shop, they found a little milk bar that did a simple tea with cakes. They settled down to relax, glad to be on their own for a short while.

'What did you think of Mr de Neve?' asked Sandy, 'He seemed artistic, well educated, yet there he was running a tiny stationers in the back of beyond.'

'I thought he had his reasons for leaving Europe,'

replied Trudie. 'One of the many who've had to leave. He's made a life here now. He belongs and seems to be appreciated.'

'I wondered who he had left behind.'

'I know. I did too. He didn't want to talk about family, did he? Think how we get homesick and yet we know we're going home.' Trudie paused, then asked, 'If things get worse back home, would you stay here?'

Sandy shivered. 'When we were driving through those burnt-out forests they made me think of those photographs you see of war, burnt-out landscapes. I really hope nothing happens while we are here – all this talk of war in Europe.'

Trudie thought of Susie's last letter, in which she had mentioned gas masks and shelters. 'We're probably just being gloomy,' she said, and changed the subject. 'Let's get a photo of the famous swimming pool. We can send it to Mr de Neve to show him we can take arty photos too, though I'm sure it won't be as carefully constructed as his.'

Their last night was spent in a modern hotel in Manjimup. It was just as modern, Trudie thought, as the very best seaside hotels in Scarborough. There was hot water in every bedroom, plenty of bathrooms, beautiful furnishings and lighting arrangements and the turkey dinner was *fit for a prince*. Their spirits had lifted and they enjoyed the company of the rest of the group. Only in bed did Trudie let her thoughts return to war. Would it really happen again? She had grown up with the horrors of the Great War. Poor Dads had been badly injured; it had affected his health and his nerves ever since. And what of Mr de Neve? What had he escaped from? She remembered the numbers of Italian and other European emigrants piling on to the *Oronsay* at Naples, bringing with them what seemed like all their worldly goods. And they were the ones who could escape. She remembered Jack saying, 'Spaniards, Italians, Germans, Jews, and all the progressive peoples of fascist Europe... what is going to happen to them? They can't all migrate.'

Perhaps Mr de Neve was one of the lucky ones?

*

A well-paved road takes us along the Blackwood River to Balingup. It is still a very beautiful drive and though we don't see the 'twenty-eights' we hear them in the trees. In Balingup we can't find the hotel where *they had lots of canaries, love birds and parrots but what caught my eye was a chocolate brown Sally. She was a darling tho' of course not as lovely as a certain golden Sally.* It must have gone a long time ago; Balingup is now a tiny village.

Like Trudie and Sandy, we think we'll never reach Pemberton as we drive through the great karri forest. We too are very grateful for a good cup of tea when we finally arrive, and avoid the imposing Pemberton Hotel. We find a little tea hut further down the road which probably isn't the same little milk bar behind the curio shop. We walk around the village and discover the pool among the trees. I still have the photograph that Trudie took and sent back home in her letter dated 24/4/38. I wonder now if Mr de Neves got his copy too. I take exactly the same view, though my colour image looks nothing like that sombre black and white snap. We walk into the forest itself to get up close to the giant trees. Trudie had enclosed the measurements in that same letter:

Girth at 5 years: 25 ft
Ht of bole: 130 ft
Total ht: 225 ft
Estimated volume 70 loads (1 volume 600 sq ft)

We walk on to the Pemberton Timber Works. Here piles of cut timber are stacked. As I look through my lens to snap them I remember my own little pile that I took from the cabinet in the attic. How I loved that shiny pile of pieces of wood that were perfect for building a doll's house. I can hear Mummy's warning now: 'Look after those carefully, dear. They came all the way from Australia. I wanted to bring home the trees but they wouldn't fit in my suitcase, so I brought home these instead.'

CHAPTER 4 – The Great Southern

THE NIGHT AFTER OUR EXTRAORDINARY DAY in the big forest we arrive in Nornalup. We've already discovered Nannup, and Trudie's Mr de Neve, as well as Balingup and Manjimup. Many Western Australian small towns end in 'up', as it is the local Aboriginal word for 'water'. Nornalup is a small one-street town on the Great Southern, where the Walpole Wilderness meets the Southern Ocean a few miles to the west of Albany. Our holiday cabin is on the edge of the village situated above the Frankland River, surrounded by blue agapanthus and the orangey-golden kangaroo paws.

This hidden retreat is the perfect place to relax and read the Albany letters again. For exercise we have our walks along the rugged coast to Peaceful Bay and Conspicuous Cliffs, where we marvel at the brilliant red ficifolia trees just in bloom. We also walk among the enormous tingle and karri trees in the Valley of the Giants. The cabin above the river is quiet, the only interruptions the calls of the twenty-eights and the firetail finches. There are no other guests.

Our host explains that it's a bad year for visitors, what with the high price of the dollar and the high temperatures earlier in the year here in Western Australia. 'Locals are going to Bali, where it's much cheaper even with the flight,' he explains. We remember that it's where Esmond and Frances Anne have gone for Christmas. Yet we are surprised to find that we have this romantic haven totally to ourselves, surrounded by the most dramatic landscape, seascape and vegetation. We have to remember that we are in a small corner of a huge continent, many hours' flying time away from the rest of the world. It's no wonder that Trudie, in the spring of 1938, felt herself *so very far from home*.

Trudie wrote more about her life in Albany over the two months she was there than she did from either Perth or Kalgoorlie Boulder. It was her last placement in Western Australia. I search my memory for any reference to Albany in the stories she told me sitting at the kitchen table on those long-ago afternoons. I can recall nothing. I remember her description of sleeping on the veranda at 'Auntie's and Uncle's'. Animal stories were my favourites: wallabies and kangaroos at the National Park. She would mimic the laughing kookaburra, rolling her tongue to make that strange clattering-chattering sound. Yet before I discovered the letters I had no idea she'd spent time on the Great Southern. These letters, though, give me more of her than any of the others.

I'm excited at the prospect of what we might discover. When I was researching in preparation for our trip, I checked all the addresses, but I couldn't find 'The Mount, Albany', on Google World. The letters suggest that it was a large house on the front, opposite the town jetty. It must still be there and we should be able to find it. I wonder now if she ever thought of it, reminisced about those days when she walked along our 'Mount' in Shrewsbury, the street where we lived throughout my childhood. I jot down 'The Mount' as the first place to locate when we get there.

Stuck in the album of letters is a pamphlet entitled 'Albany – the Hub for Holidays'. It introduces the town as 'having the most beautiful harbour in Western Australia' and recommends it to tourists for its strange rock formations and magnificent beaches. Trudie has written, in pencil, *X for places I have visited.* I note down 'The Gap', the 'Natural Bridge', 'Frenchman's Cove', 'Middleton Beach' and 'Dog Rock'. The last rings a bell and, when I check our itinerary, I discover it is the name of our motel! My stomach churns a little. Is this a good omen?

Most of the letters in the album are either to her parents or to her sister, Susie: *Dear Mumsie and Dads* or *Dear Susie* or *Dear Toozle*. She tends to use the nickname when she writes most personally. I wonder if it's code for 'don't show the others'. The exception is the only surviving letter that Trudie wrote to her brother, Alex, on 23 October 1938, six weeks after her arrival here. It begins:

Dear Alex,
Susie's last letter said 'Dad and Mum and I have just been to have our gas masks fitted'. Gosh! That gave me a nasty jolt. How are you all feeling now? I think things are a bit more settled for the present. Do you think so? We get so little news here of Europe, just scraps over the wireless, which are poor. Everyone here seems to be expecting war and some even go as far to say 'the sooner it comes the better, it's bound to come sometime.'

Albany could be made into a wonderful holiday resort but most of the inhabitants, elderly retired people, just sleep and won't do anything. It must be the climate too. It's called 'Sleepy Hollow'. The people here do seem very different from the previous Aussies I've met. They would not make a name for themselves by their hospitality.

Next week a French gun-boat is putting in for a few days so a dance is being given for the officers. All arrangements are in the hands of the Rotary Club and only members of the club get invitations which automatically exclude all visitors to the place. As it's the only dance there's been since I came six weeks ago I'm feeling a bit peeved about it. I'm hoping a miracle might happen but at present that seems impossible.

We did have one little bit of excitement this week. The Great Opperman (Oppy), the world famous cyclist, was in Albany prior to breaking the Albany–Perth record and he and his little flock of satellites stayed at 'The Mount'.

I imagine how my mother was really feeling: bored, homesick and missing her family dreadfully as they braced themselves for possible war. Susie, her dear sister and confidante, seemed so very far away. She felt that here she was at the end of the earth on this little peninsula in the far south-west of Australia. She looked out from the veranda at the Mount to *that lovely view of an almost landlocked bay* which surely reminded her of Toulon and *one of the best days ever* with her *Oronsay* friends. Yet here she knew there was nothing beyond but sea, more sea, and eventually ice. She wanted excitement, romance, fun, but she hadn't even got an invitation to the ball. However, she wrote quite cheerfully to Alex for his birthday and, knowing her brother's interest in all sports, sent him an amusing little story about the Great Opperman's visit. She described her involvement in the food preparations for the great man which she and her friends, Ena and Molly, undertook as the managers of the Mount were off to Perth. The letter ends:

What with all this and preparing his breakfast you can imagine how we were exhausted by the time the race started. But of course we were thrilled to hear that Oppy beat the record: the 254 miles had been done previously in 16 hours and Oppy did it in 12 and a half – thanks to us of course! Today another record is about to be broken, Mr and Mrs Corbin, who run the Mount, are travelling up to Perth in their little 'Bug', an old Austin Seven, and hope to make it in twelve hours.

The Uncle Alex I remember would have enjoyed these details. He was fanatical about all sports and about motor cars. He was a portly moustached businessman who went to motor racing and the horses. He ran a fleet of cars – 'Streamlined Taxis: the largest fleet in Huddersfield'. My cousin Sue and I would love to be taken out by Uncle Alex in the 'Big Bentley'. We'd 'muck about' in the back, pulling out the fold-up wooden trays and pulling down the huge leather armrest by its silk tassel. Uncle Alex and Uncle Henry, Sue's dad, would reminisce: boyhood at school, then straight into work at sixteen, 'kids don't know how lucky they are nowadays', and, most importantly, THE WAR. They were 'bore stories' to us. Born in the late 1940s, we were brought up on that phrase 'during the war...' and we just didn't want to know. It strikes me now that both my uncles had to go and get jobs to support the family, whereas my Aunt Susie and my mother managed to get scholarships for teacher training. I wonder now how Trudie's brother felt about her year in Australia.

*

The Dog Rock Motel, right opposite its namesake, is a dull place, rather a shock after our beautiful wooden cabin by the river. Our room is drab but adequate, the kind of motel room that makes you feel you could be anywhere in the world. As we unpack enough for our brief twenty-four-hour stay, I try to keep my disappointment at bay. I look out of the window on to concrete but I imagine that this section of the town would have been countryside back in 1938, the rock itself standing on a green hillside. I am reminded of Trudie's initial disappointment with Albany, despite its beauty and the wildness of the surrounding country.

The landscape is really wonderful but during the week there is absolutely nothing to do and I'm too sleepy to go for long walks. Sometimes Ena, Molly and I have afternoon tea together and once or twice, our headmaster, Mr Hill, has accompanied us. In the evenings we take a stroll round the town and if we're lucky we pick up one of the bank clerks or accountants and get taken for a run or treated to supper but more often than not we just call in at Spero's, a little Greek Cafe, and drink coffee to keep us awake. So Albany! The historical interest, scenery and natural vegetation are the finest I've ever seen but you must have gathered that the social life is defunct.

*

Walking towards the centre, we quickly lose sight of the new and find ourselves in a colonial-style town of decaying elegance. Some of the old buildings have been renovated, but many are shabby. The main streets, York Street, Main Street and Stirling Terrace, still have Edwardian shopfronts with attractive, double-fronted large glass windows, though some are now modernised, the old wooden frames replaced by steel and plastic. We discover a bookshop and wander in. I pick up a volume of historic photographs and as I flick through I discover 'The Mount'. It's a large colonial-style house with veranda and gardens. It was built originally by an early settler called William Clifton and later became a government guest house. And, evidently, in Trudie's time, it was run by the Corbins. I've roughly worked out its location and hope the 'town jetty' still exists to guide me. *You can see the town jetty quite clearly from the verandah, I've been watching the loading of a German cargo boat; it made me nervous and anxious reminding me of what's going on in Europe.* I wonder if it's on Mount Street, a little road I've noticed on my map which is off the front esplanade, Clifton Terrace. It should be easy to find. There is the little Greek café to discover too. According to Trudie, *Spero Manea knows how to run a good cafe. He's intellectual, well read, and really knows his business.*

An hour later we are exhausted and thirsty. We've looked at many of the colonial-style houses opposite the old harbour and further back on Mount Street, but none quite fits Trudie's description or matches the photograph I've seen in the bookshop. We decide to look for Spero's. If it's still a café we can have a much-needed drink, perhaps some lunch. We discover Dylan's, a little café right on the front on Clifton Terrace and an ideal place to refresh ourselves. It still has the double Edwardian shopfront under a covered colonnade. Lawrence is convinced that we've discovered Spero's. As always, he's much bolder than I am and chats away to the young woman behind the counter, telling her all about our quest. I pretend to be reading the guidebook. 'Yes,' I hear her say, 'we have an old photograph of how it used to be.' Lawrence is looking very pleased with himself as he carries the drinks over. 'You just have to ask,' he says. But it wasn't Spero's at all! The 1940 photograph shows 'The Albany Hostelry'. The young woman is disappointed too – she wanted to solve our mystery. We thank her as we leave, touched by her genuine enthusiasm.

'We're not doing too well are we? It's already past lunchtime and we've discovered nothing.'

'Cheer up,' Lawrence says. 'We've still got 'The Residency' to explore. It's a museum so it'll have lots of information. And then there's the school.'

*

The setting of 'The Residency' is exactly as I have imagined it from Trudie's description:

Oh! I mustn't forget the night Mr Butler, the resident Magistrate, came to dinner. He's an awfully nice old boy and as it happened to be Molly's birthday he took us all down to the hotel after dinner. We ended up at The Residency for a drink. It's a beautiful old house he has situated on a spit of land jutting into the bay, one of the first strong houses built in Western Australia.

I take photos of the tall pine trees, the views of the harbour and bay, and the elegant house itself. We find the entrance to the museum. I'm on the lookout for lists of Resident Magistrates. The first room is prehistory and I leave Lawrence looking at the displays of rocks and plants. I walk quickly through, finding nothing of relevance to my search. The last room is darker. It's an exhibition of old photographs of the town. I'm immediately reminded of that display in the tiny museum at Nannup and our discoveries there. This collection of historical photos takes you back to Albany in the 1930s. I photograph the photographs. Now I can see Albany through Trudie's eyes. The pictures of the famous rock formations, the beaches and the town and harbour are just like the ones in the old tourist pamphlet in her album.

I'm looking particularly for a picture entitled 'Mr Butler, Resident Magistrate'. I want people as well as places to bring my mother back to life for me, people like Mr de Neve in Nannup. But there's nothing, no pictures of Mr Butler and none of the house as it was. I almost walk out. Then I notice something: a photograph of a gunboat entering the harbour. It is flying what looks like the tricolour, only it's black and white. It's in the section labelled 'The Harbour and Port 1938'. It has to be the French Bougainville gunboat.

*

On 28 October 1938 at about 2.30 p.m. the Bougainville steamed slowly up to the twin jetty exactly opposite the Mount, where Ena, Molly and Trudie were watching from the veranda. They'd had Sports Day that morning and were given the afternoon off. As they sat watching they bemoaned the fact that they'd not been able to get tickets for the officers' dance being given by the Rotary Club.

'And we're Europeans,' moaned Molly.

'And I speak fluent French,' added Ena. 'Not that I can go anyway. I have to swot for my exam. I just have to get my degree this time'.

Trudie felt equally aggrieved: the first dance in all the weeks she'd been here and no invitation.

They were still grumbling over their tea when the phone rang. It was Spero inviting them all to supper to join his special guest from the French boat, Monsieur Henri Jules, Le Commissaire.

'Now's our chance,' Trudie told the others. 'We can charm Le Commissaire and get our invitations!'

It was two in the morning when Trudie finally got to bed and she was far too excited to sleep. They now had their invitations for the grand dance with the French officers at the Rotary Club. It had been a wonderful evening, speaking bits of French and English, talking world affairs and travel, listening to Spero quoting from Plato and arguing his socialist ideas with Henri Jules, a conservative Frenchman. She was amused to note, though, how Spero never went too far; she realised that he needed his trade with the big French boat. Ena had taken a real shine to the tall, elegant Frenchman and he had seemed impressed by her French, and, Trudie thought, by her charm too. At last, some excitement was coming to Albany!

As Molly and Trudie prepared for the dance, Ena made them promise to pick her up later if they were going on to Spero's. Trudie spent a lot of time on her hair, trying to make her fine strands bounce up. She chose her shoes with the highest heels and her best evening frock, the blue velvet with the scoop neck and low waist. Being only four foot eleven had huge disadvantages, because the slightest bit of weight showed. When she looked in the mirror and smiled, though, she felt quite pleased. Pretty eyes and a good smile at least!

What a thrill it was as the officers entered the big hall. First came Le Commandant, then the first officer, then six other officers, and then tall Henri, bringing up the rear. He had boasted about his exact height the night before. They were in full evening dress, complete with gold epaulettes on the jackets and broad gold stripes embroidered with anchors down their trouser legs, wearing their wonderful capes.

Trudie guessed that a dance with the handsome Henri was out of the question. How ridiculous they would look: the tall and the tiny. Anyway, she hadn't warmed to him in the way Ena had. But she was pleased to be approached immediately by a little lieutenant, just the right size for her, and an excellent dancer. They spoke in a mixture of French and English, and when he discovered she had visited his home town of Toulon he was thrilled.

'*C'est merveilleux que vous connaissez mon pays natal.*' His eyes sparkled and he held her closer. 'And strangely enough the setting of Albany reminds me of there, the encircled bay under the hills.' He shook his head.

'But not as beautiful,' she added.

'*Impossible!*' He laughed. '*Toulon est la plus belle cité du monde.*'

Trudie danced politely with some of the other officers, but she knew she was hoping that Gabriel would return. As she watched him dance with some of the other girls, she noticed how well he moved, how confident he seemed and how good-looking he was in that southern French way – dark skin, black hair, big brown eyes. She was excited as she watched him come back across the hall towards her.

'*Ah, ma petite anglaise,*' he greeted her, and bowed.

And then they danced all night, talking all the time. He was energetic, vivacious – laughing, talking, singing – and incredibly funny. She had not laughed so much in a long time. Molly had chummed up with Gabriel's friend Jean, a charming but rather delicate-looking Parisian, and the two officers suggested taking them out for a late dinner.

The dance had to finish at twelve. Henri Jules was keen to meet up with Ena again, so the three French officers – Henri, Gabriel and Jean – went along with the two English girls to the Mount. They started singing 'Au clair de la lune, mon ami Pierrot' outside Ena's bedroom window. After two lines they became totally hysterical, laughing and giggling, with little regard for the many elderly residents. When Ena appeared at the window

Henri cried, '*Voilà! C'est Juliet,*' which caused more laughter and giggles until someone above banged on a window. In no time Ena was with them. They ran along the front and dashed to Spero's, just in time before he closed. With his usual amazing speed he served up a supper of crayfish and toasted sandwiches.

La belle vie... at long last, thought Trudie!

*

As I stare at the photograph of the ship, I think about my mother's week with Gabriel: the parties, the picnics and the lunches on board the boat. It's described in detail to her Susie, or 'Dearest Toozle' as she calls her in this particular letter. There is so much description of every particular it's as if each single moment was of utmost importance: what they ate at Spero's, how they organised the party for the officers in Mr Hill's house, the black dress she wore to another party Gabriel took her to, and each visit to the boat, with descriptions of exactly what it was like on board. Yet what of love? Even to her sister she could not write of love, of kisses, of passion. But I can read them there, between the lines: *officers' capes are big enough to be useful* and *I don't know how long I'd been on board but Gabriel was so busy showing me the snaps he'd taken in Indo-China when I discovered it was 1.15 and I could have sworn it was only 10!*

Spero provided the six young lovers, Molly and Jean, Henri and Ena, and Trudie and Gabriel with a great 'last supper' – the boat had bought all its provisions from him! She ends the letter to Toozle:

Well we had that last supper, then we went home, and then there was our final goodbye which I won't describe to you in detail!. On Friday at 10.30 am the 'Bougainville' sailed. It was recess time and as the school is fairly high up on the hill we had a great view of her from the playground. Going home at lunch time the harbour seemed empty, the town seemed empty; no French sailors puffing French cigarettes at every corner and everything felt flat!

*

Spero's café in the 1930s   Courtesy Mark Manea

'I must find out more about the Bougainville,' I say to Lawrence as we leave the Residency.

'We'll find the library,' he says. 'We'll check out the ship as well as Mr Butler, the Mount and Spero's café. They must have records in the archives.'

'Yes, and we can also ask about the primary school. Why on earth didn't we go to the library first?'

I look at my watch and discover it's 4.30 and it's Friday. My heart sinks. 'It's bound to be closed by now and we don't even know where it is. I'm not a real researcher at all. I should have done more before we came. I should have had the library uppermost in my mind.'

Lawrence thinks he noticed the library on our way down. It's at the very top of the old town. We start hurrying up the hill, away from the harbour. We are panting and out of breath when we finally get there. We are directed to the archive section up the stairs. When we meet Sue, the resident archivist, she already has her coat on and I'm puffing so much I can hardly get out what I want to say. Who can blame her for wanting to leave on time on a Friday night? But the library is closed tomorrow. I hurriedly pull out the letters and hope I can persuade her to help.

'I've come all the way from England to try and discover more about my mother...'

I start to tell my story and gradually her impatience melts. She takes off her coat and I hand over my underlined sections of the letters. She explains exactly where 'The Mount' was situated and which building has replaced it. 'Such a shame,' she says. 'It's a horrible building now, but you'll still be able to see the view. And the Manea brothers, Spero and Cosmo, their café, the Strand, was where the little boutique fashion shop is at the bottom of Main Street. You can't miss it, it's called Shades. It's the same building exactly. They were quite famous, you know! They ran the town baths too and were well-known characters. Successful entrepreneurs and renowned for their intellectualism and radical views.'

So they really did exist, Spero and Cosmo Manea, Trudie's good friends.

Sue reads out one of the underlined sections on Mr Butler:

We were sad and bored after the French boat left but kind old Mr Butler, the RM, did his best to cheer us up. He took us for a run then back to 'The Residency' for supper. He is another lone man living in a huge house with just a cleaner coming in twice a week. Wives and families of government officials won't live in Albany if they can help it. We helped to get the supper ready; biscuits cheese and asparagus. He told us all about the Albany's big highlights that are coming soon; The Albany show and the concert in his grounds which are held every summer. We tried our hardest to sound enthusiastic and offered our help.

'Interesting social commentary, isn't it?' Sue is beginning to get involved.

She rummages through files looking for the Resident Magistrate and then she tries the archives online. She is worried that she won't find anything as the name Butler is so common and I've only got his initials: E. Y. After ten minutes of searching we feel we must let her go home.

'Don't worry,' I say. 'You've been brilliant. Just point us out the school, then we'll find Spero's and the Mount. This is fantastic. You've been incredibly helpful.'

I write down for her the few details I have regarding Mr Butler and the name of the French ship, along with my email address. She promises to look further on Monday.

*

The primary school where Trudie taught turns out to be right next to the modern library and the old school is perfectly preserved. We go first to the headmaster's house, where Mr Hill had lived: *He had a beautiful home, the best school house in the state, it's built colonial style with a lovely big entrance hall ideal for dancing.*

Mr Hill features large in Trudie's letters. His wife and children were based in Perth. He seems to have taken quite a shine to his young English exchange teacher, allowing her time off to visit other schools and even to leave early one day for her visit to the Bougainville. He let his beautiful colonial house be used for the girls (Molly, Ena and Trudie) to throw a party for the French sailors:

The next day at School Mr Hill was too funny for anything. He was in and out of my class-room all day talking in whispers – how much milk shall we need for the coffee, have you ordered sandwiches, remember the rest of the staff know nothing about the party, there's no need to tell the French boys I'm a headmaster.

And then later: *Mr Hill received us all most graciously and we all drank to the 'Bourgainville', then the fun began and thanks to Bub's marvellous playing everything went with a swing.*

As we wander round the old house, I try to imagine the party, Mr Hill *looking statelier than ever in his evening dress, the roses arranged so artistically, the three French officers in all their regalia Henri, Gabriel and Jean.* But it's hard! This old colonial house is now the teachers' resource centre. The elegant rooms are filled with photocopiers and computers. One room is set up for PowerPoint. The walls are covered with educational posters. We know it exactly; it could be the English and Media Teachers' Centre in Islington, north London.

We meet the caretaker, David, who turns out to be from Barry in South Wales. He still has a twang of a Welsh accent despite his many years in Australia. 'I still miss Wales,' he says, 'the land of my fathers and all that. You get used to a new place, making a new start, and then it's too late to go back. Of course, so many of us have come from Europe, at one time or another, looking for a better life.' I think of Spero and Cosmo.

David explains that the house stopped being used as the head's home about thirty years ago. 'Impossible to afford a grand house like this for one person. I've been minding the teachers' centre for a good while now,' he adds proprietorially. He is clearly delighted to stop and talk, and then, proudly, as if it's his own home, he takes us out on to the balcony, with its wonderful view of the harbour.

'Imagine what it used to be like,' I say, 'the huge ships in the harbour, cargo from all over world, and the French gunboat all lit up and flying the tricolour.'

The school by now is closed. It's Friday evening and everyone has gone, but we peer through the windows and wonder which one was Trudie's classroom. I read Lawrence the letter that describes her preparation with her class for the Albany show:

This week has been pretty hard at school as all ordinary work has had to go by the board to let the children do their entries for the Great Albany Show: writing, drawings, handiwork, and needlework. On Thursday all the work had to be mounted – entries from the neighbouring country schools as well as our own. On Friday morning was the judging. I was in charge of all the third standard work, forty being from my class and sixty others. Mr Hill and the second mistress did most of the judging and I was delighted that the winner of 1st prize was from my 3rd standard.

We can see the school hall where the prizes were given and where Trudie received the goodbye presentation from her class. *The children had collected their pennies and thought it an excellent idea to have the ceremony right in the middle of the school concert. I was totally surprised when Teddy made a little speech and I had to step forward. I really felt to cry.*

The building hasn't changed, though the classrooms themselves are modern and equipped with all the latest technology. I shut my eyes and try hard to imagine Trudie teaching here with blackboard and chalk, textbooks with few pictures and hard green covers, and a class of fifty primary school pupils sitting in rows of wooden desks. How teaching and learning have changed! Yet Trudie's response to Teddy is no different from how I have, at times, been moved by the affection of my students. I regret that I could share so little of this with my father and nothing, of course, with my mother.

*

After the Bougainville had sailed Trudie didn't remain sad for long. It's as if she had suddenly discovered her own attractiveness, or Gabriel had helped her discover it. The later letters from Albany are full of escapades and jaunts. There's a range of young men mentioned who take her out: Fred Mercer, *a confirmed bachelor*, then *Peter Ron and Jim* take the three girls out to a dance in the country and Jim is Trudie's partner. There's a beach party with John and Syd and there is Cosmo, the handsome bachelor brother of Spero, who is *like a Greek God* and takes her out on his fishing boat. The fun culminates in Mr Butler's outdoor concert in the grounds of the Residency to raise money for the Albany Blind Appeal.

On Monday evening we had our first rehearsal for the moonlight concert. There were about ten young people, and Mr Hill and Mr Butler. They acted as an audience and decided which songs they thought would go down well. We had a banjo, violin and a mouth organ and we made a hectic din. Mr Butler thought it was wonderful but he, like me, has no ear at all for music but Mr Hill said with lots more practice and the drama of coming across the water by boat it might just work!

On Wednesday we practised from the boats and it was a disaster. The wind carried our voices the wrong way and the back boat got stuck on a reef. Poor Cosmo had to wade through the water to rescue us. I got piggy-backed home! We felt very dubious about the actual night of the concert. However the night was absolutely perfect. The Residency and grounds were illuminated with fairy lights and their reflection in the still waters was a picture. There were several items and community singing before our little show so we anchored off the point and let off rockets till the signal was given for us to start.

We sang eight songs, some funny and some romantic. There was a gentle breeze wafting our voices ashore and we got good applause. I, needless to say, didn't sing, but I held the torch for the musicians. It was a lot of fun.

After the concert we all went to Spero's, me for the very last time. And now I've said good-bye to all my dear friends in Albany and I'm feeling terribly sad. There's been times when I've cursed Albany heartily as the deadest place on the face of the earth but it's maybe because there's so little entertainment provided that I've got to know people so well, so intimately.

I'm keen to find Spero's after our visit to the school. We follow Sue's instructions and find Shades. It's difficult to imagine it as the Strand Café. It's full of designer clothes, bits of trendy jewellery and beautifully displayed shoes. We can see what would have been the upstairs room where Spero did his own entertaining and spoiled the young women teachers, especially the little English exchangee. Modernity interferes with my imagination. It is now a stylish office with a large glass front.

Over supper in a little restaurant up the road we discuss our day's discoveries and experience for ourselves the 'small town' feel of Albany as we sit in this almost deserted restaurant and wait an hour for our pasta.

'I wonder when and why the two brothers settled in Albany,' Lawrence says. 'We have no idea if they were from mainland Greece or the Islands.'

'They could be Cypriot. Cyprus was a part of the Empire,' I muse. 'What about Mr Hill? He seems almost vicariously involved in Trudie's love life, fixing her time off her lesson so she can visit the French ship, allowing the young teachers to use his house for a party. And then he makes sure it's a pupil in her third standard who wins the prize.'

'Yes, middle-aged men on their own, without their wives here. Both the RM and Mr Hill seem to have been quite struck with Trudie.'

'She was by no means beautiful, but I think you could call her pretty.'

I get out one of the small black and white photographs of Trudie standing under a balga tree with two friends (Ena and Molly?) and we peer at it. Her hair is fine and black and pulled away from her face to show a high forehead, well-shaped brows over what I know are blue eyes. She's smiling, which shows off her high cheekbones. She is much shorter than the other two women, emphasised by their tall white 'explorer-style' hats.

'She's lovely!' Lawrence says.

'It's a shame we can't spend longer here. The library and archive are closed until Monday.' I then say thoughtfully, 'Could we stay on? I feel as if I'm just beginning to get somewhere.'

'How can we? We're expected at my cousins tomorrow. It's not fair on them to change arrangements now, especially just before Christmas.'

I know he's right but I suddenly feel slightly resentful.

Trudie and Friends under Balga Tree

The next day we drive straight back to Perth and are quickly immersed in Trinidad in Western Australia. Lawrence hasn't seen his five cousins, his old playmates, since the 1960s, when they had immigrated to Perth from Trinidad. First Elspeth and Gillian left with their young husbands and small children, then their parents and other siblings followed, Esmond being the last to arrive. Lawrence had spent his boyhood in and out of their house next to his grandparents on the hill above the gulf in San Fernando. He has hardly seen them since and hasn't been much in touch, just those Christmas round robins and the letters of condolence when parents and siblings died.

We stay with Elspeth and Richard, but are soon meeting the other cousins and their children, three generations of family. And I'm back in Trinidad 'ole talk'. The older generation speak Trinidadian as strongly as ever, while the children and grandchildren are Australians. As it's the Christmas season, we sit outside drinking puncha cremas, eating pastelles, and everyone is talking at the same time. I feel like I'm back in Trinidad, at least with the older generation. A rather 'cool' Santa Claus arrives on a motorbike with presents for all the grandchildren. The older generation are reminiscing about those Christmas Eves in Trinidad at 'Auntie Hélène's'. Lawrence's mother, Hélène, was famous for her parties for the whole family where presents were exchanged before everyone trooped off to the little Catholic church at St Madeleine.

'Your mother was amazing,' Elspeth remembers. 'It never mattered how many of us were there. We always had her wonderful Christmas Cake, well doused with rum, and those huge platters of hops and ham, and she had time for every one of us, knew all our likes and dislikes, somehow really knew us.'

'Of course she just loved the boys, Alistair and Esmond,' Gillian joins in, 'spoilt them rotten.'

The stories go on, the family fables, the time Philip fell off the roof, the time Lawrence and Andrew and Alistair and Esmond set fire to a tree. The licks the boys would get from their fathers.

'Your mother was a great storyteller, Lawrence', Elspeth remembers. 'That's who you got it from. There was a particular story that really spooked me.'

'Not the one about the knocking behind the portrait?' Lawrence interrupts.

'That turned out to be a lizard!' Gillian pops up with the punchline.

I listen amused. I know these stories so well now and in many ways feel part of this family. Trinidad has become my home too. Yet I also feel apart from them, because while they know me, they know nothing of where I come from. It's how I always felt with Hélène. She accepted me into her family but she knew nothing of mine. She wanted me to stop calling her Mrs Scott, she wanted to be 'Mummy' or 'Auntie Hélène', or even Grannie as two of her other daughters-in-law called her. But I couldn't call her any of those names because she wasn't *my* mother or aunt or grandmother. I ended up calling her Hélène.

Later that night, when we are alone, Lawrence asks me if I'm all right.

'You looked a bit sad, this evening,' he says. 'Perhaps we could have stayed longer in Albany? Perhaps we should have altered our plans?'

'No. I'm glad to be here, a part of all this. But there is always that longing for something that's gone.'

I know he understands exactly what I mean.

On Tuesday morning, after a weekend of Trinidadian-Aussie hospitality, I decide I'd better check my email. It's easy to log on at Elspeth's. I catch up on all the news from home and then I notice it:

Dear Jenny Green,
I have found 3 things of interest for you:

This article from the *Albany Chronicle* newspaper
2nd December 1938
Albany Moonlight Concert
The picturesque and historical grounds of the Residency, the home of Mr E. Y. Butler RM were utilized for a moonlight concert on the night of December 1st to augment the funds of the Albany blind appeal. Many local and country residents were present and the concert programme was presented in a charming setting. Coloured lights festooned the entrance to the beautiful drive leading to the grounds, the stately pine trees and other vantage points. The night proved ideal for outside entertainment and loudspeakers heightened the effect. A delightful feature was singing by parties in boats which slowly cruised in the placid waters beside Residency Point made historic by the landing there of Major Edmund Lockyer of 57th Regiment more than a century ago. Mr E. Y. Butler, president of the local committee, and Mr D. Collins, the honorary secretary, had the assistance of many willing helpers in a good cause.

2) From: Kythera-Family.net – for the worldwide Kytherian community.

Spero John Manea
D.O.B. 24.04.1895. Place of birth: Kythera, Greece
Date of Death: 17.06.1949. Died in W.A., Australia
Profession: Cafe Proprietor
Life Story: Spero is the son of Giannis Emmanuel Manea and Maria John Soury, born in Kythera 1895. Spero arrived in Australia aboard SS *Roon* on July 23rd 1908 in company with his brother Cosmo (born 1886, died 1964). Spero married Mona Kathleen Ward, widow, in December 1919 and had 5 sons: John (dead), Thomas (dead), Ernest, Spero (dead) and Denis. Spero took the Oath of Allegiance before Stipendiary Magistrate Archibald Parrish on March 30th 1922. He owned and ran the Strand Café in Albany, Western Australia.

3) From BlueprintBox.com MNF Bougainville 1938 aviso
Launched 21st April 1931
Sunk Nov 9th 1940
An example of fratricide as this boat, loyal to the Vichy government, was sunk by a sister ship loyal to the allies. Crew lost.

Hope these are useful.
Sue

Why are the ends of stories sad? Of course there's no way I'll know if Gabriel died on that ship. Perhaps he rebelled? Perhaps being from the Midi, from Toulon, he joined the Resistance. I can fantasise. I can hope. I wonder what Trudie knew. Did they write? Did they keep in touch during the war? Unlikely. Did she follow the fate of the French gunboats?

Although Trudie's name is not mentioned in the article about the concert I know she's there on one of the boats, not singing; like me, she was tone deaf. I know she's one of the 'many willing helpers in a good cause'. And Cosmo and Spero? Some of our questions are answered. We now know where they came from and when. Spero was only thirteen. They must have been desperate for work; nothing was on offer on the small Island of Kythera. But where did they get educated? Learn their knowledge of Plato? Was that in Greece or were they self-taught in Australia? And why did Spero die so young? He must have been only fifty-four. He too would have left young children like Trudie did. More research to do.

But now it's time to join the Trinidadians. I sit there quietly for a few more minutes, imagining Gabriel waltzing my mother round the ballroom, two young people so full of youth and hope.

CHAPTER 5 – The Traveller and the Genie

IT'S EVENING, LET'S SAY IN 1963, one of those times that we share together when Dad is back from the Windsor, his local pub. I've already had my supper, but I help him get his tripe and onions. We sit at the dining-room table. It's never laid properly, but Dad likes his rituals: he must have proper ground pepper in a pepper pot, while he's happy to eat butter from a rancid packet. We gossip about our days. I tell him the news from school, and what mark our joint effort got us for my French homework, and he has a little moan to me about Mrs Morris, his personal assistant. Of course I know how well she keeps him in check. Tonight he's quite mellow, probably has had one beer too many, and he starts on a story.

'A traveller was crossing the desert. He was alone in a great space, nothing to see on any horizon. At last he reached a tiny oasis and he stopped to rest under a date palm. He reached for a large, succulent date to quench his thirst and allay his hunger. He ate it happily and threw away the stone out into the wide space of nothingness. Unfortunately for him, a genie happened to be passing by, invisible to humans, and the date stone hit the genie bang in the eye.'

He sighs deeply as he finishes. 'That traveller is me. Somewhere along the line I've hit the damn genie.'

I refuse to indulge him. 'You're lucky to have a daughter who loves you,' I say. 'You should hear what some of the girls say about their fathers.'

This memory, which reflects so many memories of my life with Jack, comes to me now as I travel across New Zealand in his footsteps. My Jack was wise and sad and sometimes very funny. He didn't believe in God but he did believe in fate, good luck and bad. He escaped from his anxieties about being a single parent, having an invalid son and managing the hugely responsible job as chief educational psychologist through his nightly visits to the pub and through his travels. When he wasn't travelling physically he was travelling in his head, going back over his life. I can see him now, in his big easy chair drawn right up to the dining-room fire, staring into space, back in a life which had gone.

*

We discover few remnants of Jack on our travels in North Island. His descriptions of Auckland, where he was posted for his second term, resonate: *numberless little bays and backwaters, extinct volcanic craters rising from the city and the islands, as many as forty volcanic peaks, laid out parks, exotic trees, good coffee, and cosmopolitan.* He liked many of his colleagues: *rebels and intellectuals, with solid leanings to the left, what I have noticed is how well read and balanced the New Zealand intellectuals are*. But we have no names apart from a Mr Box, *one of the nicest men I've ever met, he's so wonderfully generous, tolerant and sympathetic and has a way of being able to put himself in anybody else's place first*.

There is no name given to the school where *I like the staff, an interesting crowd, one played cricket in the test matches against England in 1931. The only snag is I have fifty six children in my class. At least the syllabus is broader than at home, old Wyatt's hair would stand on end if he saw the progressive methods here!* 'The Mansions', where Jack lived in Auckland, at Whitaker Place, off Symonds Street, no longer stand. I photograph an empty space.

From Auckland he visited the northern peninsula of North Island during the Whitsun holiday, mid-autumn, May 1938, but he gives few details. It was not a touristy place then, there was no Fuller's 'Great Sights' bus tour along the ninety-mile beach to Cape Reinga with sand-boarding on the dunes, and no Waitangi Treaty House to learn about the betrayal of the Maori chiefs by the British Crown. He writes:

the Bay of Islands is glorious and totally deserted, not so very different to when Captain Cook landed! There we went by boat to a small town, Russell, once the temporary capital where the governor lived, it was like walking into the past. The hotels throughout the trip were poor and draughty. I was thrilled at one place to discover hot springs where you could bathe in the 'lobster pool' and get warm again!

In August (winter) he returned to enjoy hot springs, this time in Rotorua, but his Rotorua must have been totally different from ours. It was not then one of the most visited places in the world. His hotel, the Australia, on the corner of Tutanekai Street and Amohau Street, has long gone now. In its place, there's an ugly bakery, opposite the supermarket that is on the site of the old railway station where he would have arrived. The Blue

Baths, *the most beautiful swimming baths I've ever seen*, remain little changed, as they have been preserved as 'historic'. The black and white neo-Gothic building is impressive. We bathed there ourselves in the elegant swimming pool with its arches and fountains. I took some photographs of the old signs: 'boys' changing room', 'used togs and towels on table please' and 'fancy and scientific swimming here'. We visited the museum at the baths and looked with amusement at the machinery once used for curing different ailments. Modernity has its ups and downs! Most of the town now is new, bright and 'blingy'.

We follow Jack to Wairakei, *another geyser valley, another rumbling inferno where the geysers all play intermittingly at different intervals and the colours of the rocks are pinks and greens and reds, a strange unworldly place.* Here we saw what Jack would have seen and marvel as he did at the bubbling pots of 'porridge', the steam rising from every nook and cranny, and the extraordinary colours and shapes of the rocks stark against the bright turquoise blue of the mineral pools and the different greens of the many varieties of fern. Yet despite all this beauty, which he described and I am now seeing, I am not discovering the young man himself, not from the tip of the northern peninsula to the wharf at Wellington, where we wait for the ferry to take us south.

Our first stop on South Island is at Kaikoura, the peninsular town backed by the snow-capped peaks of the seaward Kaikoura range. We are here not to discover Jack, but to see the whales. We hope we are in luck. It

Jack's hotel has long gone

has to be good weather, as the boats won't go out if it's very rough, and I have no wish to go out even if it's just 'choppy'. And what about the whales? Will they allow themselves to be watched? Whale Watch track them with underwater microphones, but even so, we are warned, they can't guarantee a sighting; you get an 80 per cent refund instead.

When we arrive the up-to-date weather channel announces 'rough sea – seasickness alert'. I go straight to the desk, despite Lawrence's arguments, and ask to cancel. 'We'll happily refund you,' the assistant tells me, 'but I think you may regret it. You've come all this way to watch the whales and it'd be such a shame to return to the UK without seeing them.'

'When my friend came and it was that rough, she threw up during the whole trip,' I explain. 'She may have seen the whales, but it was an experience she'd rather forget.' I remember her description of puking over the side of the boat. 'Whatever you do don't take photographs,' she'd said. 'That's what started me off.'

'It's calming down as we speak,' the assistant assures me as she shows me the most-up-to-date report.

What with her persuasion and Lawrence's eagerness I have to give in. We are taken by bus to the catamaran and I'm still feeling apprehensive. Once on board I relax: it is surprisingly calm. We are overwhelmed by the views of the great bay, with the snow-capped mountains encircling it and above them that long white cloud. We look back on the strange shape of the Kaikoura peninsula. The diving whale, Taiki, that we are tracking visits the surface frequently and performs gracefully for the tourists. I wonder what she thinks. Does she even register these tiny beings with huge eyes that follow her every move? I don't feel sick at all. I'm enchanted by the huge mammal. She turns and dives back down, giving us that superb view of her tail fin as her great hulk sleekly disappears into the depths.

That night in our cabin I can't fall asleep. It's not just the excitement of the whale trip, it's also trying to remember the long-forgotten, trying to plumb the depths of my memory. I'm attempting to picture Jack. The Jack who existed before he hit the genie in the eye. I conjure up the man I knew as a little girl, before it all went wrong.

We travelled abroad first when I was just five, in 1956. We stayed at Dinard on the Brittany coast in a hotel where young English children were welcome and Madame served a special supper for the little ones. I have one particular memory of being alone with Daddy. We had gone for a walk, just the two of us, and ended up in a café. 'You're getting grown up now,' he said. 'I'm going to order you a brioche rather than an ice cream.' At that stage I was fussy in the extreme and hated all forms of bread and cakes and anything strange, but I was thrilled with my brioche. I felt so important sitting by Daddy at the café table while he sipped his magic drink that turned cloudy when you added water.

Then I see him later, after my mother died, no longer the rather trim Jack in his white sports coat in Brittany. Jack is now in his scruffy jacket with patched elbows, sitting in his big sagging chair in the dining room, rather overweight from too much beer and poor food. On this particular occasion I recall him talking to my new boyfriend, Tom Hardwicke. I'm fifteen, going on sixteen, and this is the first suitable boyfriend I can introduce to Jack. Tom is all a boyfriend who is about to meet a protective father should be. He is smart, charming and exceedingly polite. However, he is nineteen and at work, and I fear my father may still disapprove. Luckily, he has found exactly the right topic to discuss: New Zealand. Tom grew up in Christchurch and they are discussing the merits of the city and comparing it to Auckland. I'm not listening too hard as I'm not really interested, but I'm noting with pleasure that Tom is passing the interrogation with flying colours. My father is constantly worried that I might 'go off the rails' with no mother to guide me. And, of course, to some extent he is right.

As I turn over once more, trying not to disturb Lawrence with my sleeplessness, I work hard to recall any snippets of that discussion, but they have gone, lost for ever in that abyss where old memories go.

We travel across the plains to Christchurch with the Kaikoura range of the Southern Alps flanking our route to the right and the sea appearing from time to time at the side of the road to our left. It's early January, midsummer here. The mountains are different shades of brown, some still with a white cap, alight in the sunshine and contrasting with the green vines. There's no hint yet of the ripened grapes. We anticipate the pleasures of good New Zealand wine and of seeing the city that Jack described:

It's a beautiful town; the buildings are quite ordinary, apart from the exquisite cathedral, but the whole city is set among trees. The Avon, with its closely clipped grassy banks, wanders backwards and forwards through the city leaving a trail of beauty. The willows that droop over the Avon are the largest weeping willows that I have ever seen.

I'm sorry that I can't recall that long-ago conversation Jack had with Tom, or anything at all about Jack's life here in New Zealand, which he told me about all those years ago when we lived together in the house on the Mount. And Tom? Whatever happened to him? I still have a photograph of that handsome young man, and the letters he wrote to me devotedly each week while he was working in Coventry. I heard, years later, that he had gone back to live in New Zealand, returned to Christchurch, the city he had always loved.

We are spending our one evening in Christchurch visiting the home of Rod and Margot, family of our close friends in London. The evening is full of talk and laughter, good food and Marlborough wine. I tell them about my project and discover that Rod went to the famous Waitaki Boys' High School in Oamaru, where Jack gave a lecture. I read them the extract from the letter dated 2 May 1938:

Dear Mum and Dad,
There is quite a bit of news this time. First I thought you might find the enclosed cutting interesting [no cutting now]. *It is inaccurately reported of course; I suppose some poor hack had the job, but it conveys the general idea of what I said. I gave the same talk at the Waitaki Boys' High School on the following morning. Milner, the Head Master, heard the Rotary Talk and invited me along there. It was rather an interesting experience as Waitaki is one of the leading N.Z. public schools.*

'Good Lord,' exclaims Rod. 'Milner was still head when I first went. He retired at the end of my first year. He was quite an institution by then.'

What was Jack's talk about? The experience of an exchange teacher or the situation in Europe? I wish that cutting had not disappeared. In other letters he talks about lecturing on the German situation: his knowledge of that country, his hatred of fascism, tempered by his belief that not all Germans were Nazis. He loved the German language; he was fluent. He visited Germany as a boy and as a young man. 'Until 1933,' I explain, 'when he saw for himself the rise of fascism – broken windows, racist graffiti and fear.'

Rod suggests that we visit the school and see if there are any archives that may contain references to the lecture. 'It would be fascinating to know how people here responded to his views,' he says.

We discuss researching the local newspapers. Katrina, Rod and Margot's daughter, is experienced with archives and warns us that many old newspapers are not yet digitised. 'It takes days to plough through microfilm,' she tells us.

We feel exhilarated as we say our farewells – the good company, the wine, talking to New Zealanders, and a tiny step towards discovering Jack. Even that thought, though very tenuous, that Rod knew Milner who knew Jack. It's a beautiful night, completely clear and warm. We stroll along the banks of the Avon and see Jack's grand weeping willows, presumably still the same trees. Under the huge spire of the cathedral we try to imagine Jack standing here, but he's retreated into the shadows. The Orari guest house, where we are staying, is quite close to the cathedral. It's a colonial-style building with arches and balconies right in the centre of the city. Luckily it was not remotely damaged by the last quake, unlike the girls' high school just across the road, where we see huge cracks and bits of tumbled wall. It seems to be the luck of the draw.

After a full breakfast at the Orari of fruits and cereals, eggs and toast with home-made jam, and a quick check for emails on the free wi-fi, we say goodbye to the friendly owners and find our route out of Christchurch. We travel south to Oamaru, the opposite way to Jack.

I managed to scrounge a ride by car from Dunedin to Christchurch. The train journey is slow and tiresome and

I'm glad I managed to get the lift. It's a lovely journey by road across the brown Kakuni hills, all wrinkled and folded with blue shadows in the furrows, then on to Maheno where the willows are now yellowy gold, stopping in Timaru for lunch, then a glorious view across the plains to the Southern Alps.

The Southern Alps are on our right, now browns and buff, not the autumnal green Jack saw, but the subtle colours of summer. The sea is on our left. We stop every so often and dash out of the car with our binoculars to look at seals and seabirds, hoping for a glimpse of the blue-eyed penguins. The weather is still sunny and warm.

On first impression time seems to have stood still in Oamaru. It's a quiet town, beautifully preserved, with all its original buildings standing. Jack described it as

A prosperous little town by the sea. It has a wide main street with a double line of trees down the middle. The streets are pretty and grassy. The railway line crosses the street. It's funny to see the express puff across the main road without any level crossing, only the loud clanging of the bell.

We park close to the railway crossing by the old station. It appears that only the clanging bell has gone, replaced by up-to-date signals. The wide main street is still tree-lined, with grass and flowers between the pavements and the road. We walk up the hill to discover Bay View House, Wharfe Street. Jack wrote to his parents from here on 5 March 1938:

Such a short time in Dunedin; no sooner in it than out of it again. When I finished up at my first school, where I had a very fine time, I was told to come here 80 miles North of Dunedin. I am staying on the hill, overlooking the town; the house has a pleasant verandah in front with a glimpse of the sea; and the road is planted with rowan trees, now full of their red berries.

All the houses now have numbers rather than names. What I had imagined would be easy, when I googled Oamaru at my desk at home, is now a challenge. We walk up one side and down the other, looking for the right period, checking for a veranda and making sure there's a view of the bay. After a process of elimination we decide on the one that was probably Jack's. I take a multitude of photographs, some of the house, some of the view. Does it really make any difference whether it's the correct house or not? I remember the gap where Mrs Woolcock's house once stood in Cottesloe, the disappearance of 'The Mount' at Albany, the demolition of The Mansions, Whitaker Place in Auckland. I'm always just a step away, not quite there, somewhere round the corner.

Just round the corner, in fact, is where Jack taught. The school is an old building with modern extensions. On the old gatepost is engraved a memorial:

> IN MEMORY OF EXPUPILS AND TEACHERS WHO
> MADE THE SUPREME
> SACRIFICE IN WORLD WAR II
> 1939–1945

I think again of my father here in 1938, just one year before. He would have known some of the above. I read out Jack's brief description: *The school is a pleasant one full of well behaved, well fed children. I have about forty five twelve year olds, boys and girls.*

'I do wish he'd given more details of his actual teaching,' I moan.

'His letters certainly are brief and perfunctory, but his audience is his parents. Remember my letters back to my mother? 'The only place to live in London is Chelsea.' I was sending an illusion, an idea of my life, not the real life.'

Lawrence is right but I feel unexpectedly angry with my father. Why are there no descriptions of his teaching? Of his pupils? Of his colleagues? Lawrence has a bundle of letters that he wrote back to his parents in Trinidad during his years away. Letters his mother kept and gave back to him at the end of her life. These regular letters home to Trinidad are full of details of that time in London, even if romanticised. He gives snapshots of his young teaching days in Peckham: his excitement at discovering so many students from the Caribbean, his determination to discover the appropriate Caribbean literature to take into the classroom – stories by Sam Selvon and poems by Martin Carter. Then his own early poem: 'To the Poet's Mother.'

I remember my teaching time in Trinidad, now teaching Caribbean literature myself. I had longed to be able to write to Dad and tell him all about it. He had followed every step of my young teaching career, even during his last long illness. Sharing ideas on education had been our close bond. Living in Trinidad, three years after his death, I still missed him so much and longed to share all my new experiences. Yet Jack told his parents virtually nothing about the school curriculum here in Oamaru. I can learn nothing of what he actually taught, only how many children there were in a class.

We look down on the town and the harbour from the hill above and guess that it has hardly changed at all in seventy years, yet the view alone can't take us back there. Jack's letters, so different from Trudie's, give us so few people.

'I do find it odd,' I say to Lawrence, 'because the Jack I knew was such a "people person", though he wouldn't have expressed it like that. We loved a good gossip. We would analyse everyone! And, more seriously, my Jack was so interested in education.'

'But he was a young man here. He'd not yet studied psychology, and I guess he was a bit of a dreamer, and quite wrapped up in himself. What he wanted most of all then was to be a writer, yet he's not sure quite how to go about it. I remember how that felt!'

Lawrence remembers too the feelings you hide from parents when living abroad. The stories that you don't tell. He guesses at Jack's disappointments. Certainly homesickness and loneliness, and maybe even boredom. 'After all,' Lawrence adds, 'Oamaru must have seemed, especially then, a million miles from Forest Hill in south London. It was a "dry" town for a start and we know how Jack liked his pint. And he was a Londoner, used to theatres and cinemas and, well, just life!'

'Yes,' I say, 'and he was half the world away, or many weeks on a boat.' I look at the sea, its endless miles and only Antarctica ahead. 'No quick escape, no brother, like you had, to pay for your passage home.'

We're hungry. It's a long time since that brilliant breakfast! We have heard good reports of Fleur's restaurants; her food is famous in this part of New Zealand. We set out down the hill back to the old port to find the Loan and Merc, which is Fleur's new venture. Here in an old converted warehouse the new restaurant specialises in meat. It offers an excellent buffet lunch of cold plates and salads.

'It must have been hard,' Lawrence suggests, 'moving from school to school. Jack was only a few weeks in Dunedin, then he's sent here.' He looks carefully at the dates. 'He arrived in New Zealand on 4 February and was writing from here a month later.'

We have the photocopies of the letters spread out on the rustic wooden table.

'Yes, we hardly hear anything about that first school, but I think it's the same one he returns to in Dunedin: St George's. It's always hard, however good the kids are, when you start at a new school in a strange place. Remember our experiences.'

That time as young teachers in Trinidad, we had so much wanted to teach in a village school by the sea, up at Toco, on the north-east coast, but the Ministry of Education had other ideas.

Lawrence recalls his miserable year in the boy's Catholic grammar in San Fernando. 'That awful drive every morning from Port of Spain and, when I was late, reported to the headmaster by a boy in my own class, the class monitor.'

'And it took you over a year of badgering the ministry

to get to Aranguez Junior Sec, and everyone thought you were mad to leave Presentation College, yet you were over the moon when the transfer finally came through!'

'It did take us a while to settle into Trinidad. Remember that first term when we both found it hard to make friends? I think it was the same for Jack. He sounds much happier in the later letters.' And he reads out:

I feel now as if I've lived here for years, London seems to exist now only as nebulous and shadowy. Oamaru has become my focal point. I can't walk along Main Street now without meeting half a dozen people that I know and there is certainly no safety here in the seclusion of the cinema where I'm bound to bump into my pupils!

and

I shall always remember Oamaru for cycling and picnicking during warm autumn weekends, bathing in rivers, oyster suppers and a host of pleasant friends. Someone took me up to the mountains one week-end in a car. The roads were terrible, wide, dusty and stony but we had amazing views. The mountains are bare and wild, no grass just tussocks and stone. The light was very intense and I loved the contrast between the blue water of the lake and the pinky haze of the mountains. We spent the night in a lonely mountain hut, just a pallet of straw to sleep on, and a roaring fire to keep away the cold. It is grand country side, it has a power about it, a wild lonely expanse.

'Isn't there a photograph of Jack camping in the

mountains?' I rummage through the file to find the tiny black and white snap. It's difficult to make out the face: it could be Jack or it could be a friend. The figure looks relaxed, stretched out in front of a campfire, smoking a pipe. On the back is a faint date in pencil: 15/3/38.

'Relaxing in the outback'

*

Jack stood on the veranda looking out over the harbour from his boarding house, Bay View, on Wharfe Street. The rowans were bright with their red berries. There was promise in the air. It was warm directly in the sun but with the southerly blowing there was a chill. He had grown to love Oamaru. He enjoyed his teaching and all that was going on at the nearby South School, with the enthusiastic boys and girls. But this morning he was not preoccupied with the work he did with the smaller children. Through his talk at the Rotary Club he had been invited to give a lecture at the well-known Waitaki Boys' High School to the masters and senior pupils. He was going to talk about Germany. He found that, understandably, there were misconceptions about Germans in this small town. People's views were tarnished by what they were hearing about Hitler and his National Socialism. Jack wanted to tell people that what should be resisted at all costs was fascism but that this should not be mixed up with hatred for Germans and German culture. His mind flashed to a memory of his first visit to Germany in 1924, when he was studying German for his 'highers'. He had stayed with the Wettermans in Hamburg. They had seemed so very cultured and had introduced him to modern German literature. He had discovered Gottfried Keller and Ferdinand Meyer, Swiss writers whom he still read. He sighed. He was now quite apprehensive about how his views were going to be received.

As he made his way along the main street with trees down the middle, the breadth of the centre of town gave him a sense of the openness he was going to require of his audience. He had been talking at breakfast with one of the guests who had blown in for the night. 'You won't find your views popular. They are gearing up for war. You'd be surprised how many of the young men are thinking of joining up.'

He hated talk of war, jingoism was how he thought of it, yet on the other hand fascism had to be fought. As he walked along the main street towards the big school, he remembered his last visit to Germany in '33. The signs were already up: '*Juden verboten*'. The family who he had stayed with regularly during his youth refused to discuss the political situation. He felt they were sympathetic to his views but frightened.

He looked up at the grand sign, 'Waitaki Boys' High School' as he walked through the imposing gates. The school looked like a replica of Dulwich College. He felt intimidated as he made his way up the long drive. He remembered his own disappointment when he hadn't got the scholarship to Dulwich and had gone as a second best to Wilson's Grammar School, Peckham. Now he was glad he hadn't had an education with 'toffs'. He identified with workers. Socialism could succeed. He was impressed with the socialist government here in New Zealand. 'I'd better be careful how I present my views,' he thought to himself.

He arrived in the school hall with the gracious Mr Milner to find a large audience: older boys, their parents, teachers and officials. He felt sick with anxiety as he walked on to the stage. As he got to the microphone his nerves vanished. He would do justice to his views. He wouldn't talk against war, as he himself felt it was a necessary evil, but he would try to explain how this situation had arisen in Europe and remind them of the fact that nearly half of the German people were not Nazis.

His young friend from school, Peter, picked him up after the talk and they made straight for the mountains. It was just the relaxation that Jack needed after his challenging ordeal. The road was narrow and rough and the car bumped along, but Jack didn't mind. He was thrilled by the open expanse of country, the wildness and loneliness of the place. They camped in a little wooden hut and there was a well-organised place to build a fire.

'So the talk was a success?' Peter asked as they settled down to smoke their pipes after supper.

'They were certainly a sympathetic and attentive audience, but the questions I was asked at the end gave me the impression that I'd not really moved them on the key facts. They believe that all Germans are self-aggrandising, that all really do love the Führer. I think they believe we should wipe out the whole damn lot!'

'Well, better than the opposite,' Peter remarked. 'I'm even considering the possibility of joining up if there is to be war. What will you do, Jack, when you return?'

'I have no idea! It seems that the world has truly gone mad. I can't imagine myself as a soldier. Perhaps if there is war I could work for the Intelligence agencies. After all, I am fluent in German! My simple ideas of social equality seem to have no place any more. I certainly need to settle to something when I leave here. I'm thirty and have achieved so little.'

Jack sighed as he thought of all his dreams coming to naught, but he didn't really want to explain to this kind New Zealander his disappointments in himself, in love, in his career, as well as his deep anxieties about fighting a war.

They sat quietly, smoking in comfortable companionship.

'I wonder what we'll both be doing in ten years' time,' mused Peter. 'I guess I'll still be teaching at South School, and I hope I'll have met a really nice girl by then. You'll have to come back and pay a visit!'

'If the world doesn't spin out of control, I promise I

will,' said Jack.

That night he dreamed of Joyce. He woke in the early morning to a feeling of overwhelming sadness. He wanted to return to his dream, to hold Joyce close, to make love to her. 'Will I never get over her?' he thought. He knew there was no hope. That was why he'd come here, wasn't it?

He heard her voice: 'Jack, my dear, I can never love you in the way I should. I have a friend, a lovely girl, who will make me happy.'

When she had finally told him it all made sense. And, of course, he couldn't hate her for it, though he had wasted ten years of his life hoping. He understood fully why she'd tried so hard to love him. 'You can't love when the desire is just not there,' he told himself. He knew that too. He could see little Trudie Landsborough looking up at him with those pretty blue eyes of hers as they danced on board the *Oronsay*. He liked her so much, but where was the passion? He wondered if he'd ever feel it again. 'I'm so lucky to be here in this beautiful place,' he told himself, 'to be travelling the world,' but he knew he really wanted someone to share it all with. 'I want to be lucky in love,' he whispered to himself as he stood gazing into the bush on this lonely hillside somewhere in the Southern Alps.

CHAPTER 6 – Otago

AS A CHILD I HAD PRESUMED that everyone apart from my older brother, who was a communist, believed in God, as I did. I went to a Church of England school, loved scripture and enjoyed being an angel in the nativity play. When my mother was ill I prayed regularly to God to make her better. After she died, I imagined meeting her in heaven.

I don't remember having discussed God or Jesus or heaven with my father. It's strange, now I think about it, as we discussed so much else in those first years after my mother's death. Dad must have been deliberately avoiding the subject, perhaps not wanting to shake my belief in what was comforting me. He must have understood that I was imagining a heavenly reunion with Mummy and Grannie Annie. He never discouraged my visits with friends to a variety of churches and youth clubs. One day, when I was in my first year at the Priory Girls, I was doing my routine job of picking up and sorting the post. Lots of journals arrived for Dad and usually I'd just stick them on one of the many growing piles of 'in mail', but this time I happened to read the heading: *Ethical Record*. I was curious, having just learned the meaning of the word *ethics* and when he got home I asked him what it was.

'It's the quarterly record,' he explained. 'It's from the South Place Ethical Society, which is a bit like church without God. It's where I went when I lived in London.

Our social life was Conway Hall. We had dances and entertainments, bridge club and concerts. Your grandmother played the piano, your Uncle Sydney organised the entertainments and your grandfather was the treasurer.'

'Don't you believe in God, Daddy?' I asked after I had digested this family involvement in something that was like a church but wasn't.

'I'm an agnostic,' he said. 'It means I'm not sure.'

My own faith waned gradually, despite my wanting to believe. By the time I was a sixth former, I loved discussing ethics, philosophy and humanism with my father. Many of my friends enjoyed it too. As the mid-60s hit us, social life at the Methodist youth club became boring. Late-night discussions at 111 the Mount, after the pub, became the norm.

My father died when I was twenty-four and, at that age, I had no idea how to organise a funeral so I arranged for a member of the Ethical Society to conduct the ceremony at the crematorium. Yet I had never visited Conway Hall. There are many references to people from the Ethical Society in Jack's letters. He and his parents discussed the politics of the society and the members, and every few months they sent him the *Record*. He writes to them of submitting articles on his travels. I needed to read them. So before we left on this trip I decided that I must visit the South Place Ethical Society, still located at Conway Hall, Red Lion Square, Holborn.

The library is upstairs. It's an old-fashioned room, dusty, musty and full of glass cabinets of books and papers; a library from an earlier age. It can't have changed much since Jack was a regular member. The librarian apologised for the lack of digitised material – 'Just no funding,' she explained. 'There are only obituaries online,' she added. I was shocked at the enormous files of *Ethical Records* she showed me, a hundred years of the magazine. I wondered how I'd ever find the articles I was looking for.

'My father and his family were all members,' I explained. 'My grandfather was the treasurer for many years.'

'I'll see if we have their obituaries,' she offered. 'Just give me the full names of your family members.'

I scribbled them down quickly before beginning my search. I eventually found the file labelled *Ethical Record 1935 to 1940* and hunted from February 1938. At least I had some rough dates. It was the May edition before I found anything: *Mr J. L. Green in New Zealand*. It began: *I'm puzzled by the fact that many of you have not heard of Oamaru.*

I smiled to myself. I wasn't at all puzzled. I doubted that many people now, even in our technologically speedy world, have heard of Oamaru.

*

Now, as we drive away from Oamaru on our short journey to Dunedin, I dig in my research file for the article and obituary. When you read about a place you haven't yet visited it just washes over you. When you've actually been there it comes back to life. The Oamaru piece ends:

I can think of one scene which will always express for me this part of South East New Zealand. It is evening and we are travelling on a small dusty road. On each side spreads the plain, and beyond it the hard wrinkled hills. Everything is bare, there is little rain this side of the Southern Alps. The earth is covered with patches of tussocks and it looks as if hundreds of little porcupines are sleeping on the ground, everything is silent except the noise of our car on the rough road. Suddenly we come upon a great flock of sheep being driven down the road ahead; dogs bark, dust flies, there's a scuffle and some bleats, then once again we are alone, just the plain and the blue hills. That's New Zealand and it's lovely.
Oamaru April 9th 1938.
Jack L Green

It touches me, seeing Dad's name there in print, reading something he wrote so long ago, when I've just been in this landscape myself. I wish I could tell him about being here. I look again at the obituary that the librarian had found for me. I am now struck by the ending:

Jack was a linguist and a great traveller who made friends easily in many countries, a connoisseur of good food and wine. He understood modern youth, earned their respect and numbered many of the younger generation among his friends. He was never too busy to give his attention to problems of others. A loyal friend who will be missed by many.

Which friends from New Zealand did he stay in

touch with? If only I'd found his old address book too, as well as my mother's. If only I'd looked more carefully at all those old letters kept in the boxroom in Shrewsbury before I did the big clear-out in 1974. I do have the names of two friends in Dunedin from the letters: Professor Findlay and John Harris, both from the University of Otago. I hope I can discover something about them. And then there's mention of a local schoolmaster Jack visited:

The next week-end I was invited to a place called Shag Point. It's on the coast half way between Oamaru and Dunedin. It's a haunting wild spot. The sea birds gather in thousands on the rocks. I stayed with the schoolmaster, a very clever fellow who hopes to come to England to do his PhD. He's a socialist and a strong supporter of the Labour Party here.

I reach for our map and eventually locate Shag Point. It's actually just off our route to Dunedin. 'Look out for a sign to Shag Point,' I tell Lawrence. 'It's just after Katiki, east of Palmerstone.'

We are about halfway to Dunedin when Lawrence shouts out, 'Look, a signpost. Shag Point.'

We drive along a little road to a small, empty car park. We find a shaky wooden gate that leads to a cliff path. Lawrence is ahead and has the binoculars. He's shouting something, but I can't hear. The wind is carrying his voice away, while the crash of the sea and the cries from the seabirds are drowning the rest. At last I make out 'blue-eyed penguins'. I rush along and grab the binoculars. Yes, there they are! Wonderful little things, all over the rocks out in the sea beneath us. You could hardly find them with the naked eye they are so well camouflaged, black against the black rocks, their tiny blue eyes hardly visible even with the binoculars. I know we are lucky to see them. The guidebook says they only come ashore at dusk.

Thank you, Jack, for bringing us here. It is, as you say, *a haunting wild spot.*

Otago is the southern Maori word for red earth. It became the name of the old province, centred around Dunedin, and it is still used today for the region. We are staying on the Otago peninsula at Broad Bay, just a few miles from Dunedin. The owners, Jules and Lutz, have given us detailed instructions on how to find the cottage and the key. It is a gingerbread house, hidden behind trees and thick foliage, but just yards from the sea. The garden is overgrown, a mass of colour at this time of year: the red flowering pohutukawa and the white flowers of the manuka growing wild, and someone has planted blue hydrangeas. We retrieve the key from its hiding place in a peg basket by the back door and let ourselves in. We inspect the cottage eagerly; we've had good reports.

It's tiny but has everything we could need. The kitchen is just big enough for the two of us. The design is retro, so the bread bin and cheese board, the eggcups and saucepans, all remind me of home, real home in Shrewsbury, apart from the fact that everything shines. It is scrupulously clean. The bedroom is all bed; it's white and frilly with a crocheted cover. In the living room there are landscapes and seascapes with Maori motifs. We remember that Jules, like many New Zealanders, is partly Maori. Through the window you can just see the sea and the land beyond, if you peer hard between the flowering trees and shrubs. It feels like a little holiday within our holiday. We open a bottle of local wine and sit out on the wooden bench.

We wake to a sea mist. We can't see much through the cottage window now, and out in the garden the views of Dunedin and the peninsula have gone. It's cold and damp. The cottage seems less romantic in this weather and definitely chilly.

'We can drive up to the end of the peninsula,' Lawrence suggests. 'It may be a coastal cloud.'

I'm pessimistic and in a bad mood. I get like this when I'm disappointed and revert to being a child. But what else to do? When you're on a tight schedule you can't just sit and read. I think about going into Dunedin, but the library will be closed on a Sunday. We set off on the coastal road, driving away from Dunedin towards the tip of the Otago peninsula. At the end is the royal albatross sanctuary. After a few miles we turn a bend in the road and hit sunshine and a view of hundreds of tiny islands. I look back and can see the mist hanging there behind us. Lawrence is pleased with himself for having made the decision to come. The road climbs steeply as we reach Tairoa Head, the albatross colony. The clouds have kept visitors away, so here we are on this spectacular point all on our own. Above us are birds that seem the size of light aircraft. I had said to Lutz, 'How will we know the albatross?' and he'd just said, 'You'll know.'

We are feeling smug and lucky again. The perfect spot in perfect weather and we have got it alone with the royal albatross. I now understand 'The Ancient Mariner'. I had never imagined a bird so huge. No wonder it was such a curse to have it hanging round your neck! Although it's very sunny, there's a strong wind and we begin to feel cold despite the wonder of the giant birds. We jump back in the car, ready to explore the rest of this eastern, cloud-free, end of the peninsula. As I pull the door shut a gust of powerful wind wrenches it the other way. And now it won't shut at all. It's 'kaput', as Dad used to say. We drive straight back to Broad Bay with me holding tight on to the door.

First we phone the Omega car rental company. Lawrence has to wait for ages to get through, while I am searching an old phone directory for the AA or equivalent. When Omega finally answer they tell him that no one can possibly reach us to look at the car until midday the following day, at the earliest. We try the AA, but no help is available in this remote corner, not on a Sunday. Finally Lawrence reluctantly rings Lutz. He's with us in no time with his friend, Dave, who 'understands cars' and brings with him 'just the right kind of spanner'. A 'twenty-eight', Dave says. In New Zealand, apparently, a twenty-eight spanner is famous for 'just doing the trick' and so it does! They manage to close the door so it can open again.

On Monday morning it's raining. This is our one day marked for Dunedin. I'm hoping to discover Jack's digs at 21 Glencairn Street, which is *up on a hill with a view of Signal Hills in front of me and a view to the side across the town to the ocean beyond, and five minutes walk from George Street school.*

The library may provide the cutting from the talks at the Rotary Club and the Waitaki Boys' High School which we hadn't been able to research in Oamaru as the school was shut for the summer. There are also Jack's friends, Professor Findlay and John Harris, whom he would meet regularly at *the very good bookshop where everybody seems to meet on Saturday mornings. Nobody ever seems to buy anything. You just stroll round, look at the books, and chat.*

Lawrence is hoping the bookshop still exists as he's wanting the chance to do some book browsing himself.

Although it's cloudy and drizzly as we drive into Dunedin we are determined to carry through our plans. Lutz has told us that the south side of the Otago peninsula is clear today so we decide to drive back that way later and explore what are said to be the very best beaches, Hooper's Inlet and Sandy Point, in the sunshine. Apparently the weather here is very local.

We find the house on Glencairn Street right at the top of the hill. Jack was good at choosing places with views. It is quite run-down, a grubby shade of yellow with paint peeling off the doors. I imagine it's not changed much in seventy-odd years. The views are not so wonderful either today in this rain. There's certainly no *ocean beyond.* We photograph the house rather self-consciously. It looks empty but you never know. At George Street School, which is, as Jack described, *five minutes away,* we find little remaining of the original building. I remember my thrill at South School in Fremantle when I discovered the photograph of Trudie's pupils. There is nothing like that here, not even the remains of an old stone wall.

Dunedin looks grim and grey in the rain. I imagine it that autumn of Jack's visit. It must have seemed very bleak at times. It was a 'dry' Presbyterian town, no pubs to while away the time in and watch life go by, which Jack loved doing in London. No cafés in which to sip a glass of wine, as he would do in France. The Lonely Planet describes it now as 'a surprisingly artsy town which has more great bars, coffee shops, and eateries than its small size deserves, enjoy a teapot of cocktails at a messy student pub!'

Back then in 1938 Jack wrote:

the atmosphere of the place seems an Americanised provincial Scottish town. There are cinemas, milk-bars, cafes and pie-cart shops in the American style, there are buildings, monuments, and churches in the Scottish Presbyterian style. There are some ugly buildings in the town itself but the hilly suburbs are lovely. It's quite bleak when the wind blows.

He felt homesick at times during his first few weeks. He missed his family home in Dulwich, his brother Sydney, his neighbours, the Miller girls, Phyllis and Muriel, and his dear friend Joyce. He felt lonely, even as he began to make friends. He needed intimacy. Although he was thirty, and very independent, he missed his mother.

When I look back on our life together in Shrewsbury I can see how very lonely he was at times then. The invitations to dinner with colleagues and their wives stopped after my mother died. He'd go down to the pub for a couple of hours most nights, while I'd go round to one of the neighbours. He had his drinking pals: Ron Hough, the primary school head, 'Old Lid', the eccentric philosopher, and Dougie, the journalist on the local paper. It would have been all male talk: politics, sport and the quality of the beer. He must have missed that constant companionship and intimacy that he had shared with my mother. When he'd get back home, though, that's when we would talk. I learned from him the pleasures of analysing people.

Back in Dunedin of 2012 we follow the Lonely Planet's tip and warm ourselves up with an excellent caffè latte in one of the smart cafés near the Octagon rather than opting for 'a teapot of cocktails at a messy student pub'. Then we find the library. We are directed upstairs to meet Lorraine, the local archivist. I start by showing her the quote from Jack's letter, hoping it will involve her in our research: *I don't know if I mentioned before but Dunedin Public Library is one of the finest in the world. I should just like to show the Dulwich Librarian around it. It might shake him out of his complacency a little.*

She laughs and says she hopes it lives up to our expectations. She shows us where to search for references to key people and where to look at the microfilm from the old papers. Lawrence takes on the dreary work of ploughing through old copies of the *Otago Times* on microfilm to find the piece which was in the missing cutting about the lectures at the Rotary Club and Waitaki Boys' High School. I research for any references to John Harris or Professor Findlay. I know that Professor Findlay, Professor of Philosophy, was president of the local Left Book Club. Jack attended the meetings and social events. I soon locate a reference and learn that he left Otago after the war and returned to South Africa. It is Lorraine who discovers some articles on John Harris, the man Jack described as *quiet and unassuming but very bright, and extremely radical*. He was well known for setting up and running the Otago University library between 1935 and 1948. He spent many years at the University of Ibadan in Nigeria, where, according to the articles, he played a crucial role in building up the new university. In 1967 he became the vice-chancellor. I wonder if Jack kept in touch with either of these two academics after he returned to the UK. Did they ever know how he changed from that rather shy and idealistic young man who wanted so much to be a writer to become a pioneer in educational psychology and child guidance? My father was a modest man who never thought much of his own achievements. He would have looked with admiration at the successful academic careers of his two old friends.

Lawrence has no luck with the microfilm. There is no mention of a Jack Green, a visiting teacher from the UK, giving a talk at the Rotary Club. The sun is out at last and we have learned by now when it's good to just give up on research. We thank Lorraine for her amazing help and support. Like Sue in Albany, she just got 'stuck in' with us. She has explained exactly where the bookshop used to be on Cumberland Street. 'It was three floors of absolute chaos, books, magazines and papers everywhere, great piles of books on the floors, on the window seats, but people loved it.' It certainly sounds Jack's style. As we walk down Cumberland Street, I picture my father surrounded by all those stacks of books and papers at home in Shrewsbury. We take a photograph of the large building where the famous bookshop used to be before we set off in the sunshine for those beaches on the Otago peninsula.

Jack's bookshop once home of the 'Left Bookclub'

*

One Saturday, towards the end of his stay in Dunedin, Jack left the bookshop on Cumberland Street and turned right towards George Street School and home. At first he didn't realise how cold it had got. He was deep in thought, replaying his various discussions. Had he put forward his views clearly about the European situation? Had he fully understood what John was saying about true radicalism? Did he just seem wet behind the ears to these chaps who had already come up against the authorities for their political beliefs? He envied his friends their certainties. As he passed the university he realised just how cold he was. Winter was fast approaching. Perhaps it was as well he'd be travelling north soon. Auckland was mild in winter. Then the thought of making new friends all over again hit him! He turned up Union and on to George Street and as he passed the school he thought how comfortable he'd been there. No, it wasn't as delightful as South School in Oamaru, but he'd got to know his form now, all of the thirty-four boys and eighteen girls in the top class. He'd really worked at it and now, again, it was all change. As he began to climb the hill up to Glencairn Street he suddenly felt incredibly homesick. That longing for home opened up the wound that was his old longing for Joyce. He would break all his self-made promises about only writing occasionally. He would write to her the moment he got out of this cold wind and managed to warm up again.

21, Glencairn Street,
Dunedin, Otago

May 2nd 1938

My Dearest Joyce,
I received your last letter and poem. Thank-you. How I miss your company and so often imagine you here with me. No don't sigh! I know how you feel only too well but I must express my thoughts.
   I saw Deanna Durbin in 'Mad about Music' the other day, what a delightful film! Have you seen it? I should so

much like you to have been there with me to discuss it after, as we so often have, after a good film. The WEA is thriving here and I saw 'Mourning becomes Electra', very professional, I thought.

It took a while before I made friends but now I have met some wonderful people. No not a young lady, as you so unkindly suggested I should do in your last letter, but a few very interesting men. Chaps who have the same views and values as myself, firmly on the left. The university librarian John Harris was a Rhodes and Carnegie scholar. The last government, the Coates administration, who showed nasty little Faust tendencies, got the police to warn him that if he took the scholarship he would never get another job. Luckily they were totally defeated at the last election. As I think I explained the socialist government is doing well. John is quiet and determined. He will go far. Then there's Prof Findlay who runs the Left Book Club. I've been to the meetings and socials and met a like minded group. Some of us meet in the local bookshop on Saturday mornings, like today.

Last week I was invited to Shag Point by the local schoolmaster there. It reminded me of Cornwall, but for the seals and penguins. (Remember that week we spent at St Ives?) He and his wife entertained me well. He's a bright fellow who came out top in his MA last year in all NZ. These clever men! Makes me think I have more academic work to do. Perhaps take another degree? I can't do much with my German nowadays can I? Unless I become a spy!

I have had little time for writing, Joyce. I marvel at your discipline. Sometimes I feel so very disappointed in myself. Not only in our love, my dear, but in my own paltry achievements. I did get off a brief piece on Oamaru for the Ethical Record. Look it out if you can.

No, I have not heard from my 'little boat friend' as you call her, rather unkindly. It is probably because I have not written and sent an address. Best not to encourage where you don't want to go.

I have not fully told you about my Easter trip to Lake Manapouri but that can wait. Soon I shall be on my trip to see the North East and West of South Island, then on to North Island and Auckland. More of this wonderful country to discover. And another school to settle into before the end of May. Please write to me soon, dearest Joyce. I have made some good friends here, as I said, but at times I do feel lonely.

I will send on my Auckland address, and forgive me for being:

Your ever loving,
Jack.

He didn't address the letter. Writing it was enough. He didn't want Joyce to know how much he still longed for her. Instead he wrote to his parents, telling them very much the same news but missing out the personal stuff, no mention of his longing for Joyce, no mention of Trudie Landsborough. If he could just write to his mother it would be different. He wanted to be home in Dulwich, talking to his mum. He saw her as she was at the family goodbye party for him, at the piano playing a duet with her sister Winnie; they're singing one of their favourite folk tunes, 'Maxwelton braes are bonnie, where early falls the dew, and it's there that Annie Laurie gave me her promise true'. He blinked back the tears: this was pure sentimentality, he had to get a hold of himself, this nostalgia, this *Sehnsucht*, was no good. He got up, strode to the window and looked out to hills and water, the Otago peninsula glistening in the distance. I'm so lucky to be here, he told himself, in lovely Otago. He went on looking at the view while humming 'and for bonnie Annie Laurie I'd lay me down and dee'.

*

We leave 'lovely Otago' in cloud and mist. While Lawrence drives carefully with the headlights on, I am trying to remember those conversations I had with Dad about Joyce. It strikes me now that he never seemed ashamed of the fact he had loved her for so long before he met my mother. And I don't think I felt jealous of her on my mother's behalf. I was intrigued. Later, when I was at university, I had a friend Dad always said reminded him of Joyce. She was tall, slim, athletic and incredibly bright. She was rather aloof, 'cool' was our word of the late 1960s. I envied her that 'cool' and the way the boys always fancied her, wanting what was 'hard to get'. When I recall her as she was then I think of Joyce.

We turn south towards the Catlins and the end of the world, and drive towards brightness and light. Now we are moving away from Jack's domain and going to the furthest tip of New Zealand. It's a different landscape again: little hills, deep forests, lakes and seascapes. The coast is rocky, the stones black; nikau palms and Norfolk pines grow at the edge of the road. There is evidence of petrified forests, strange rock formations where the old trees once grew. We are in an ancient landscape looking south to the South Pole. There's nothing between the breaking waves, the band of black rock, the splash and spume of white spray, and Antarctica.

Studio Cottage, Curio Bay, is built on the beach. We look out from our picture window to dunes, tall grasses, clumps of harakeke and wild lupins. Beyond is a long beach, then the sea. You can't help wondering if the sea ever comes up and covers the cottage, drowns it, before it recedes. The cottage is hunkered down among the sand hills, secret yet seeing.

We walk straight out, across our lattice sided veranda, on to the beach. No footsteps here of Jack or Trudie, just the large prints, right along the beach, of some big animal. We follow the footsteps until they disappear into the sea and walk on, through a small campsite, to yet another beach. We learn from the tourist information on a wooden board that this is the spot that the yellow-eyed penguins love. It's a perfect place to hide their babies while they go hunting for food. Luckily we are here at about the right time: early evening, before dusk. We sit and wait and before long the first one arrives. It's fun watching her progress on her rock by rock, jump by jump, journey up the beach. Nothing or no one will stop the penguin reaching her young, hidden in the rocks. The next one arrives, then the next, one by one up the beach, posing for photographs on their way. As we watch, the beach begins to fill and flashy cameras abound. Despite the notice requesting visitors to keep their distance, the hunt for the perfect picture takes over. I'm beginning to worry that the last penguin will never reach her baby.

It's time for us to leave.

As we retrace our steps back along the shore I notice a very large-looking seal ahead. We exclaim together, 'A sea lion!' Lawrence pulls out the binoculars and we share them to watch the great galumphing animal make his way back to the sea. We give him time to get right in before we move on, as we have read that sea lions can be dangerous. 'Never go between a sea lion and the sea for the sea is their escape.' We almost bump into another couple, so intent are we on viewing and walking. They are the only other walkers on the beach and are also gazing through their binoculars. We stop to exchange views on sea lions, fur seals and elephant seals.

'Have you ever seen such huge footprints along a beach?' the guy asks.

I think about footprints as I look down at the sand. How long does a footprint last?

I lie in bed sleepy after such an energetic day but unable to sleep. My thoughts return to Jack. I think of him at the bookshop in Dunedin discussing the New Zealand Labour government with Professor Findlay and John Harris. They are adamant that Labour must win the election that is approaching and stay in power. Jack tells them how impressed he is with the economic situation here under this radical government. I see the young man getting excited, glad to have found like-minded people, socialists, agnostics, readers, philosophers.

Then I remember my Jack, Jack in his early sixties, my age now, sitting with a crowd of young people at home, after the pub. There's the gang from the Priory Boys: Pete, Keith, Kid, Dick, Willy RT, Walt and Geddis.

There's us, Mount girls, Sue and me from the Priory and Pen from the High, and Sue's mate Sheila, who's in her class. We're all discussing politics, life and whatever young people discuss. Jack is part of the group, the honoured member. He has found his place here in Shrewsbury with the 60s generation. For them he's a bit of a guru. He may not like their music but he likes their ideas. Shrewsbury life has stifled Jack with its conservatism, both politically and socially, but now he has found his niche through his daughter's friends.

I remember those words from the obituary I discovered in the library at Conway Hall: *He understood modern youth, earned their respect and numbered many of the younger generation among his friends.*

In the morning we wake early to the light pouring in. Our bed has the whole view of sky and dunes and sea. You just want to lie here for ever and gaze at the changing light. The present is too magical to leave, the two of us cocooned in this secret world.

CHAPTER 7 – Trekking and Tracking

TRUDIE LEFT PERTH ON TUESDAY 7 December 1938 to travel east. So much had happened in the year, so much had happened in the last few weeks at Albany. She was laughing and crying as she waved from the deck of SS *Orford* to her family below. When would she meet them again? Uncle John and Auntie Alice, Dick and young Isabel. The cousins had promised to come to England as soon as they had saved enough, but it seemed unlikely. It was so far to travel at such a turbulent time. She gave one final wave as they turned to go.

As the ship moved speedily out of Fremantle harbour, she made her way to the stern and watched the coastline. She was trying to spot South Terrace School, but they were too far from the coast. It was closed now for the summer holidays and Christmas. Trudie hadn't arrived back in Perth as early as she had intended, so she never paid a last visit. She felt a little guilty, as she had delayed her return to spend as long as possible in Albany. She shivered. It was getting chilly now. Although it was late December, there was a cool breeze and the sun was setting fast.

Despite the sea being choppy around the Bight, she slept through the worst of it and spent the next couple of days relaxing and catching up on her letters home. She wanted time to reflect on all that had happened in those last wonderful weeks in Albany and prepare herself for the challenges that lay ahead: the Milford

Track walk, and travelling through New Zealand on her own before arriving at Uncle Charlton's in Wanganui. Apart from a couple of sets of deck tennis and a few games of quoits with Sandy, she kept herself away from the social life of the ship.

The SS *Orford* stopped for a day in Adelaide, where the weather turned cold, windy and wet. A huge cloud of depression began to descend on Trudie. Life had felt so perfect in Albany. This journey east felt wrong. She was leaving behind in Western Australia so many precious new friends: in Perth, in Kalgoorlie, and in dear Albany. Now Sandy would be leaving too, once they reached Melbourne. She hoped Bridget, who was leaving Sydney, would also be on the *Maunganui* to New Zealand. Although they had corresponded fairly regularly, neither had communicated their final plans or made a definite arrangement to meet. It was all very well planning a trip on your own, but the thought of exploring South Island with no companion and with an unknown group of travellers suddenly felt daunting.

The depression didn't lift as they set sail for Melbourne. The sea was the roughest she'd experienced since the Bay of Biscay and she had to retire to her berth for twenty-four hours and concentrate on not vomiting. The nausea brought with it an intense feeling of homesickness. She wasn't sure, though, where she was homesick for. Was it for home itself in Fitzwilliam Street, for Dads and Mumsie, Susie, and golden-haired Sally? Or was it for Claremont and her cousins? Or was it for Albany? She imagined sitting in Spero's café with Cosmo and Jim. She wanted to be cuddled and hugged. As she felt this physical desire her thoughts returned to

Gabriel. It was only three weeks ago, but he was gone for ever. 'I just don't want to be an old maid,' she thought. Sometimes it seemed that her world was made up of old maids: Miss Iverson, Miss Ryan and Hilda Burnside in Perth, Bridget and Sandy, her fellow exchangees, and Margaret Petyt and Muriel Cocking, the two teachers from Bradford who went on to New Zealand. Even at home it was the same: her sister Susie, now thirty-four, her old schoolfriends, Bunty and Debs, unmarried, her colleagues and friends at school in Birmingham all still 'Miss'. She was twenty-eight, *a spinster* as it said on her passport. Twenty-eight and she'd never had a really serious admirer. 'I'm just like Anne Elliot in *Persuasion*,' she reflected. 'Where is Captain Wentworth?'

On arrival at the harbour of Melbourne she discovered that her trunk had gone missing. Instead of joining Sandy on the city trip to Melbourne itself, she had to spend the day in the offices of the Orient line at the port. Eventually, the capable Mr Willis promised to make sure that the trunk got to Auckland before she set sail on the SS *Monterey* on 10 January on the journey across the Pacific. She just managed to make it back to the SS *Orford*, to see Sandy off, before it sailed. Looking at all the passengers bound for Europe, she felt a strong desire to join them. She hugged Sandy goodbye and they promised to write and meet up back in Britain. They had shared so much.

'I'll never forget our trip into the Great Forest,' Trudie said.

'Nannup and Pemberton! They seem a million miles away.'

'Write to me, won't you?'

'Of course!'

To stave off the mounting feeling of depression and loneliness, Trudie booked herself into the grand Victoria Palace, which Hilda Burnside had recommended. She felt like an American in a film as the bellboy carried her luggage to the elegant room. She fumbled uneasily with the tip, not sure how much to give. She was delighted with the piping-hot water and the huge bathtub. In her smartest dress, she explored the lounge, the lady's boudoir and the hairdressing salon. She had fancied having her hair done until she checked the prices. So she strolled out into the evening, which was very much warmer than Adelaide, and felt thrilled to be in a big city again. After all, Perth, delightful as it is, really only plays at being a city.

She spent an hour in a news theatre catching up on the worrying stories from Europe; Hitler was threatening Poland, Franco was winning in Spain. Fascism was on the march. She didn't want to think about it, yet. As she came out of the cinema she spotted a smart café and treated herself to toasted asparagus rolls. She wondered if they had this delicacy in New Zealand too. Her depression and anxiety were disappearing as she thought about the journey across New Zealand and meeting her relatives in Wanganui.

On her way to the post office the next morning she heard a familiar voice.

'Is it really Trudie?'

There was Bridget! They stood in the middle of the pavement holding on to each other and laughing.

'I've just this minute got off the train from Sydney!'

Bridget exclaimed.

'I'm so glad you've made it. I was keeping my fingers crossed.'

They spent the day sightseeing and talking, catching up on their year's exchange and planning the next adventure.

'It's all come and gone so quickly,' said Bridget.

'My last night on Australian soil.' Trudie sighed. 'I wonder if I'll ever come back.'

*

'Manapouri – Lake of the Sorrowing Heart'

I am thinking about my father rather than my mother as we set off on our pilgrimage west to Milford Sound via Lake Manapouri. We have travelled from Curio Bay in the Catlins via Invercargill, picking up Jack's route in Lumsden, a little town right in the centre of southern South Island. In his letter home, written on 2 May

1938, he describes his Easter trip west from Dunedin to the coast:

Lake Manapouri is lovely; peaks jumbled up all around it and the bush comes right down to the water. In the lake there are numberless bush clad islands. It is pure romantic scenery of the mournful Celtic kind. It is called 'The Lake of the Sorrowing Heart' – Manapouri means that in the Maori language. The lake is completely unspoilt. The only habitation round all its miles of shore is the guest house. There is no road round the lake; in fact the bush is practically impassable.

It's certainly a romantic description, like the young man himself, but surprisingly accurate even in 2011. We stay the night in a functional motel overlooking the lake. There are few other guests. We pass no one as we walk around the lake in the evening. It seems as unspoilt as in Jack's description. The evening light after a sunny day shoots a mass of colour over the surface of the water. We walk through shady pines with glimmers of silver light from the water touching our path. We come upon a small marina, Pearl Harbour, an idyllic, peaceful spot, despite the irony of its name. There are a few boats tied up at the little jetty. The trees grow right down to the water's edge and are perfectly mirrored in the clear lake. We stand and listen to the sounds of nature, water lapping, birds calling, rustles in the trees and undergrowth.

But now, suddenly, we hear voices. We are back in the busy world of tourism. A large party is arriving, clambering off a coach, voices full of excitement. They climb down on to the tiny jetty, filling it completely. They are leaving by boat to cross the lake. I remember now that this is where you can set off for Doubtful Sound, one of the most popular tourist destinations in Fjordland. We wait for the boat to depart, eager to claim back our solitary space. I am glad that Manapouri itself has not been developed, at least not yet. It's how the young Jack must have seen it seventy-three years ago, with his own longings, his own sorrowing heart.

The next day we pass through commercial Te Anau and up the Eglinton Valley, following in Jack's footsteps. My mood has altered from the joy of the night before to depression. The weather has totally changed. The cloud is so low that we can't even get a glimpse of the mountains. Lawrence tries hard to cheer me up: 'Enjoy it as it is. See the mist over the lake and soak up the atmosphere.' He opens the windows to let the sounds come in, but I only feel the cold air. I am experiencing a deep sense of loss and disappointment. How ridiculous it is to chase after dead people! The whole project seems suddenly absurd. I get out Jack's letter once more to see if I can regain my enthusiasm for my search but the words mock me: *It is a lovely valley; the sides are a tremendous height and the mountains tower into the sky.*

I reach stoically for the Lonely Planet and read about the journey to Milford Sound, marking the beauty spots where we should stop. At Mirror Lake there is no mirror, just a large group of tourists from a bus taking snapshots of the non-reflecting lake. A little later we follow the sign to Lake Gunn and I notice there a small sign saying *Cascade Creek*. This must be exactly where

Jack had camped: *There is lovely bush in the base of the valley at Cascade Creek camp where we stayed nestled right in the bush by a rushing creek.* I wish he'd said more in this letter. Who was he with? Did they walk the whole valley? How long did they stay?

We walk through the red beech forest, passing the creek and on to the shore. As we look out from the dense vegetation into the lake we can see the light changing. The lake is shimmering, turning from silver to blue. I laugh at myself, at my childishness. I reach for Lawrence's hand. 'Sorry for being so silly, so moody. I so much wanted a perfect day and now it seems to be coming.' We stand there in the quiet watching the light change as the huge mountains appear above the Eglinton Valley.

On our drive over the mountains there are signs to the Milford Track. Strange to think that the Milford Highway, this road celebrated for scenic beauty, and the Homer Tunnel itself, were only completed in 1940. My mother had to walk the track; she had no choice. Did she too explore the chasm where the Cleddau River plunges through boulders eroded over thousands of years into extraordinary shapes? What pluckiness travelling across New Zealand, largely on her own, back in 1938, before it was one of the world's great holiday destinations. We are following slowly behind a group of Japanese tourists who have arrived just before us. We wait for their photography to be completed so we can have this scenic spot to ourselves. The majority of the group click-click and go but a few linger like us, enchanted by this weird unworldly place.

*

Trudie and Bridget set sail on the *Maunganui* on 17 December 1938, sad to be leaving Australia but excited by thoughts of seeing the famous sights of New Zealand. They both taught geography and wanted to see for themselves some of the greatest wonders of the natural world: the fjords, the glaciers, the high mountains and the thermal lakes.

The crossing was beyond all imagination. The sea was certainly rough, but the boat itself had a peculiar swaying, rolling, turning movement, like an old tub jam-packed with people. Not everyone on board was especially clean, nor were the washrooms. Trudie and Bridget retreated to their tiny berths. It was daytime and Trudie couldn't sleep. While the boat lurched and her stomach churned, she tried to think of all the beautiful things that had happened since she'd left home. That had been Jack's advice when the *Oronsay* first hit the Bay of Biscay. Seeing her looking green, he had said, 'Go up on deck, look at the horizon, and dream the best things in life.' Dear Jack, he was a dreamer. She wondered where he was now. Yes, she was going east towards him, but how unlikely it was that she'd see him. He would have already done all the great sights in New Zealand. He was probably on his way home on the *Oronsay* with the majority of the other exchange teachers. The school year had ended... Why would he stay? Especially given the worsening situation in Europe. And he'd never written. She remembered clearly giving him the Claremont address before they landed at Fremantle. She had hoped that they might have arranged to get the same boat back, then travel together across the USA, but that seemed unlikely now. He would be well on his way.

No, she mustn't think about Jack. But it was difficult not to! The day in Ceylon, that trip to Kandy, it was one of the best days of her whole life. Why did her thoughts always return to him? She forced her mind back to dwell on her little romances in Albany. She'd never felt so admired. She'd never looked so good as she did with that tan – the first time she'd ever got really brown. The romance with Gabriel had given her confidence. He was so amazingly attractive and also such fun. Then that last brief summer flirtation with Jim. He wasn't a replacement, but she had been flattered by his attentions. She missed Cosmo and Spero too. She had for a moment thought Cosmo was interested in her, but now she wondered if he was that interested in girls at all. Sadly there was no Ena or Molly to discuss this with or gossip about the dear RM and Mr Hill. She giggled as she remembered the night of the 'Albany Moonlight Concert'. But Jack was who she really wanted. It was not just his good looks and charm either, it was his vulnerability. She felt a strange need to make everything all right for him. 'Silly,' she thought, 'when he doesn't seem to want me.'

'Land ahead!' The cry woke her from her dreams. She hurriedly dressed and went up on deck. Black mountains rising steeply out of the water with their white peaks glittering in the sun and their steep sides shrouded in cloud, what a magnificent sight it was. As the ship approached the black changed to green, for they were thickly covered with vegetation from more than halfway up. Closer and closer the ship crept to the inhospitable-looking barrier. Trudie could see no sign of an opening. The sea had calmed and the sun was shining, but she still imagined being battered against those mighty peaks. Yet the boat seemed to know its business. It veered to the right a little, passed a tiny white lighthouse, then went sharply to the left and, suddenly, there stretched a long arm of the sea moving inwards towards land, mountains rearing up on either side, their snowy caps reflected in the still waters. Numerous waterfalls dashed down the steep sides.

'A fjord!' she shouted to Bridget, who had come to join her.

'Look!'

Bridget pointed to a colony of seals sunbathing on a flattened rock just a few feet away. After a while, ahead in the distance, they saw a small stretch of cleared land and they could just make out a building. As it came into view, they realised it was their Milford Hotel. The boat stopped and dropped anchor and they saw the small launch which had been sent out to meet them. Just fifteen passengers got off, all with rucksacks, and they descended like a troupe of performers down the wobbly gangway into the little craft. Amid cheering and waving, the boats separated, the *Maunganui* making a large circle before heading back to the open sea.

'Poor passengers,' Trudie said, laughing. 'I feel a different woman now.'

*

Milford Sound through Trudie's eyes

We take our trip on the fjord in the quiet of late afternoon after the majority of visitors have left. It is, in fact, about the same time that Trudie landed, *so happy and relieved to get onto dry land, so pitying of the passengers who stayed on board.* Her descriptions of the fjord come alive for me as we travel towards the ocean and back: the towering grey peaks, the rushing waterfalls, the bright green lower slopes, the immensity of the place. As we turn around in the open sea I too look for the gap in the wall of peaks, and like Trudie can see none. Even the tiny white lighthouse is still there. Back in the fjord on that *long arm of the sea* the seals are warming themselves on the rocks, and I try to get them and the full height of the cascading water in my lens. It is more fun without the camera. I put it away as the boat pulls up under a waterfall. As the water splashes off the rocks and on to my face I think about that brave young twenty-eight-year-old here, in landscape that has not changed since she saw it, apart from the slow erosion of ancient rocks.

We have supper in the restaurant which was once the Milford Hotel. There is a display of old photographs on the walls. They are of the construction of the Homer Tunnel 1938/9: the workers preparing the mountainside, digging the tunnel, paving the road. Trudie may well have seen those same workmen we are looking at. The Milford Track passes close by the tunnel before it veers off into bush.

*

Afternoon tea was served as soon as Trudie and Bridget arrived at the Milford Hotel. Both women tucked into the sandwiches with gusto, appetites revived. They chatted with a Mr Cummings, who let them know he was author of *Australia Calling* and was here to take a coloured movie of the Milford Sound and Track.

'There'll be fewer walkers soon,' he said, 'once the Homer Tunnel is complete. You are lucky girls to see it now in all its unspoiled beauty.'

'I hope you'll be walking in our party,' Bridget said, flirting with him.

But Trudie was relieved when he said he was filming the Sound first. She didn't fancy a three-day hike with this pompous, self-satisfied chap.

They spent the evening watching the light change on the water, watching the stars appear, and Trudie thought she'd never been anywhere so beautiful. She wondered if this magical place really would be spoiled by the opening of the tunnel and the road. And then her mind drifted to Jack. Had he been here too? Hiked the Milford Track from Te Anau? She hoped that some day somewhere she could share this with him. Yet just suppose he'd not yet left New Zealand? Suppose he was visiting Te Anau for a final trip?

Bridget broke into her thoughts.

'Time for dinner, my dear. It's the last hot one we'll have for a while! And it's a 9.30 start tomorrow.'

'I'm so excited,' Trudie said. 'Aren't we the lucky ones!'

*

That night, in the backpackers' lodge, I can't sleep. The day has been exhilarating yet sad. I want so much to reach back to those two young people, who themselves had been divided by space and time, at their moments here. Jack was in his camp at Cascade Creek in April and Trudie was walking the Milford Track some eight months later. Did they share these thoughts and memories with each other in their later years?

CHAPTER 8 – Puzzling World

THIS MORNING, after a rather interrupted night's sleep at the Milford Sound Lodge, we go out at dawn and take yet more photographs of the granite peaks with their waterfalls, the dark blue water and the little harbour. Over our simple breakfast of cereal we wonder which was the group of young backpackers who kept us awake. We leave briskly as now we want to avoid the arrival of all the coaches. We follow our trail back through the Homer Tunnel to join the Eglinton Valley. This time Mirror Lake reflects the high mountains and the golden trees: the distortion in the lake makes the mountains even taller, their peaks curving in the ripples. The wide valley – The Flats – shows off the huge peaks of the Livingstone Mountains. There are not many cars on the road, yet, but we can see three hikers on the horizon making their way along part of the Milford Track. From this distance it could be Trudie, Bridget and their travelling companion, except that they passed here so long ago. It's strange to think of them right here! They hiked through the forests, over the mountains staying in simple wooden huts.

Bridget, myself, and a laddie from New South Wales set off along the road which eventually, when the Homer tunnel is complete, will connect up with the Eglinton valley road. What wonders of nature this will open up to people who cannot do the walk and it will not in any way spoil the track for it follows quite a different route. The walk itself was beyond all expectations in every way, the magnificent scenery, the company, and the accommodation which includes food. The weather was perfect, not a spot of rain before we finally reached Te Anau.

Te Anau is where Trudie stayed after her three-day hike. There was just one hotel then. It was here she would have had a chance to recover from the strenuous hike and reflect on her achievements. And it is here she would have collected her post, which included the letter from Dads dated 30 November 1938 which I found in the old album along with all her New Zealand letters. It begins with the news of his cousin's death:

My ain wee lassie,
First things first. You will be very sorry to hear that my poor cousin William has died. As you know he has been fighting ill health a wee while now.

It also, at the end of the letter, suggests their shared love of hiking.

Good progress with the knee. On the Saturday I followed the course of the Bogery Burn right from Betty Knows by Hill-head to Five Mile Course where it joins Loch Foot Burn then I walked on to Dumfries, the going was very rough and it commenced raining before I got into Dumfries, but the knee stood up well. On Sunday evening I took the Norton climb to the top of Johnny Turner's, the evening was clear and I could see Cripple and a large portion of Solway; lochs lying away in the distance; and the

Galloway hills towering upwards almost reaching the sky, but best of all I could see the little farm with its neat little croft like fields, stone enclosed, which became our landmark on that memorable day's outing when you so heroically triumphed over difficulties. Perhaps when you come back we might do Cripple to Queensberry hills; I have intended doing that for years but always get stranded. Last year I definitely set off to climb Cripple but found there was no ferry boat to cross the Nith.

Well dearest wee daughter my gem of pure joy, I hope you enjoy your great walk along the Milford Track and come home safe.

Fond love,
Dads

PS Remember 'The Banks of the Nith' by Robbie B.?

The Thames flows proudly to the sea
Where Royal Cities stately stand
But sweeter flows the Nith to me
Where Comyns ance had high command...

How ever lovely the Milford Trek don't forget your homeland!

My mother clearly learned to love hiking from her father. She and Dads walked together on the Pennines near Huddersfield, and in the Southern Uplands in Dumfriesshire. To me, as a child, he was a bit of a puzzle, as the grandfather I knew never quite lived up to my mother's stories of him. I called him 'Grandad-in-Huddersfield' to distinguish him from 'Grandad-in-London', of whom I have no memory at all. But Grandad-in-Huddersfield I do remember, just. I can see his dark glasses, his moustache and his walking stick, and I can hear his Scottish accent. I found him rather frightening, a wee bit strange. What I remember much more clearly are my mother's stories about her adventures with her father. She'd often reminisce when she was baking shortbread or scones, or beating the batter for Yorkshire puddings. This was the food that reminded her of home. I loved to imagine her as a little girl walking across those hills round Crocketford. Climbing to the top of Johnny Turner's. Crocketford seemed a wild, romantic place and I longed to go there. As she told her tales her accent would get more northern, slipping between her Yorkshire brogue and the southern Scottish dialect of Crocketford.

Now I have been able to imagine her hiking the fifty-three kilometres of the Milford Track along the valleys of the Arthur River and the Clinton, joining our route near Lake Te Anau.

Now Te Anau is heaving with campsites, cabins, motels, hotels and cafés on every corner. It is a tourist hub, the centre for exploring the Fjordland National Park. It is not the pretty place that Trudie stayed in to recover from her blisters. We decide not to stop ourselves and continue our journey east and north towards Queenstown, following the exact route Trudie took in her *Service Car* with Bridget, the NSW *laddie*, a young man from Victoria, and a Mrs Tricks,

the sort of bore one occasionally meets when travelling who has been everywhere, knows everything and tries to find out all one's business. At first she greeted me as a long lost friend when she heard my name was Landsborough. 'Oh you're one of THE Landsboroughs are you?' She said 'I know the daughter of the Queensland explorer very well, she lives here on South Island.' And so she rattled on. I could see the two lads looking totally bored. I got in eventually that I was a Dumfries Landsborough, from peasant stock, though she's still convinced I'm a close relation to the explorer! Apart from her the run to Queenstown was delightful especially the latter part where the road follows the shore of Lake Wakatipu with the Remarkables on our right – a truly remarkable range of mountains.

The road along the lake on the edge of the mountains is pretty remarkable too. The weather is perfect today and we keep stopping at the little parking bays to enjoy the views and take pictures, though my camera does little justice to the wide sweep of scenery and the growing view of Queenstown as it begins to take shape on the horizon. We haven't yet had lunch and we are hoping to eat in Trudie's hotel, Eichardt's, which, according to my research, is still there, just on the edge of the lake.

We are starving by the time we get into Queenstown. It's jam-packed with traffic and difficult to find anywhere to park. Both of us are irritable, nagging and picking on each other, through hunger and driving fatigue. Eventually we find Eichardt's. Now it's an upmarket shopping plaza as well as a hotel. I hadn't picked that up on Google. The restaurant is 'fine dining', not suitable for us at this particular moment; we are sweaty, tired, moody and ready to eat a large amount of cheap food. We find a café nearby and begin to pick up the vibes of Queenstown. It's modern, groovy and loud, a paradise for young people. There are ads everywhere for white-water rafting, bungee jumping, river surfing and white-water sledging, flying gliding and skydiving and jet-boating. This is not our scene at all! We decide to head out as fast as we can.

I've discovered on the map a small road to Wanaka over the mountains above the Cardrona River. It's probably busy in the New Zealand winter as there are ski lifts, now unused. In late January, in the height of summer, there is no one on the road but ourselves. As we begin our descent we see Lake Wanaka strung out before us, a long lake with four fingers and a thumb. It looks a most beautiful place to meet the son of my mother's cousin Gordon. He's my third cousin, I guess, or second cousin once removed: Stuart Landsborough. Gordon's father, William, and Trudie's father, Thomas (Dads), left their homes in Crocketford and came together to Huddesfield around the turn of the century to make a living from the cloth. They started off as 'credit drapers'.

I wonder what Stuart and I will have in common, three generations on. First, though, we must find our bed and breakfast homestay. This sort of accommodation is a new experience for us. 'I'm not sure I like the idea of being right in someone's home,' Lawrence worries as we pass the sign 'Welcome to Wanaka'. I'm busy deciphering the instructions. Eventually we come to Harper's, a very pretty house up a long drive at the edge of the town. Our hosts, Jo and

Ian, greet us warmly and take us up to our room. It is very attractive. Everything is in pale blue and white, and it smells of flowers. It has a good view of the mountains and the lake. However, it is quite small and situated right off the living room. It's the kind of room that makes you feel you mustn't mess it up or make it grubby, or have an endless night of passion.

We are invited to tea in the living room to eat home-made scones and jam and cakes. Over our tea we get to know each other. Jo, it turns out, was once teaching in north London as a supply teacher so we share stories about teaching in the ILEA of the 1970s. We know the names of the schools she taught in. Of course they've changed names now, amalgamated, become academies or closed down. She wouldn't recognise them.

'So why have you come to Wanaka?' Ian asks. 'Most visitors just drive through, stopping off at Puzzling World on their way to Queenstown.'

I explain that it's not Puzzling World itself that we've come for, but the owner, Stuart Landsborough. 'He's a distant relative of mine. Do you know him?'

'Everyone in Wanaka knows Stuart. He's larger than life! Not physically, but he's a character. He's put Wanaka on the map with his amazing maze. He's brought tourists to the town. He's helped our tourist trade in a number of ways. A clever, inventive man, likes to go his own way.'

Lawrence catches my eye. This evening might prove quite daunting.

Jo and Ian give us directions to Stuart's house and I ring him to let him know we are on our way. His emails have sounded friendly enough, but I still feel a little nervous as we walk through a magnificent garden to a well-designed modern house.

'Hello, distant cousins,' he greets us with a chuckle. 'Welcome to Wanaka.'

He pauses, then says, 'I've never had any interest in family stuff. I leave all that to my brother Drew and my sister Bonny. You've met Bonny, I gather?'

I attempt to explain how we are related but he soon jumps ahead, before I've got past great-great-grandfather William, our common ancestor, and his two sons, Alexander and John.

'How did you find *me?*' he asks.

I briefly describe our project and my research. I'd discovered mention of some New Zealand Landsboroughs in Trudie's letters so I had googled the name Landsborough and had rediscovered Gordon, *a prolific writer and publisher*, on Wikipedia. Here, in the entry about Gordon's life, Stuart himself and Puzzling World were mentioned.

'I checked the website but found no address, so eventually I asked a young friend, Zelda, who lives in Wellington to find and send me a postal address. I didn't want to approach you on email. The rest you know.'

'Yes, I probably would have ignored an email. I got Bonny to check out that you were kosher, the real thing, a real Landsborough. We've had all sorts of odds and sods pretending they're related to us.'

Over a fish dinner above the lake, we get to know more of Stuart and his life, and the history and success of Puzzling World. He is a generous, creative, expansive man but, I gather, not particularly interested in his roots.

'Bonny will fill you in on the family stuff, and my eldest brother, Drew. He even wrote a book on the Landsboroughs. Don't see myself what the fuss is about. Our side of the family were small tenant farmers in southern Scotland for generations. We're just peasant stock.' He grins and flexes his healthy muscular arms. 'We did meet the other lot once, the descendants of the famous Australian explorer. Nice people, a good time, but we didn't keep in touch.'

Stuart insists we be his guests at Puzzling World the following morning and although we have a long journey ahead, going over the Haast Pass to the west coast, we allow ourselves to be led into his magical land, children following the Pied Piper. We enter a huge world of make-believe where we shrink and expand, fall forwards without falling, sit in Roman baths with Romans, lose ourselves in a miraculous maze, puzzle over optical illusions and play extraordinary games. Our

host leads us through his masterpiece with the enthusiasm of a connoisseur. He is an inventor/magician par excellence.

It is only as we are leaving, and are already much later than we intended, that he suddenly says, 'Oh yes, I've got something to show you.' He goes to the boot of his car and fetches an album. There are old photographs and jottings. 'You see how my father felt about Huddersfield,' Stuart says as we read: *I wanted to leave Huddersfield as fast as possible after my father died in November 1938. It held nothing for me. A dirty depressing place full of narrow minded people.*

I look at the photographs, small black and white snaps. There is one of a large family group. As I peer at the tiny faces, I recognise my grandfather, Thomas Landsborough, and next to Thomas a young teenage girl, very slight. Surely it is Trudie? I wish I had those pictures with me, the two I have at home of Trudie as a girl.

I go to the car and pull out my documents to find the right letter.

'Look', I say to Stuart. 'This was written by my mother just after your grandfather died.'

I was so very sorry to hear of the death of Willie Landsborough. How terribly sad for his family, particularly for his son. If you should see Gordon please send him my love and sympathy.

'Yes,' Stuart said. 'My father was extremely close to his father, but not to his mother. He left Huddersfield for good straight after his father died. But that family story you will have to get from Bonny!'

Before we leave I take photographs of the front of the site, with all the brightly coloured crazy models, the 'leaning tower of Wanaka' and the huge sign 'Stuart Landsborough's Puzzling World'. Coachloads of tourists are arriving. It is time for us to hit the road.

'I hope we'll meet again,' I say.

'Maybe, but you'll have to come back here!' Stuart smiles and waves us off.

I hadn't told Stuart about my mother's feelings for her second cousin. I remember her telling me how, when she was a little girl, she'd hoped to marry her cousin. I do know that they went to school together at Royds Hall and that she always spoke about him with pride. The boy who made it as a writer. I grew up intrigued. Then I forgot about his existence until I found the references in my mother's letters. It was strange reading on Wikipedia about his life in publishing and writing, then thinking about the snippets I once knew. I searched through all our books, now housed in Lawrence's study, and found *Tobruk Commando* by Gordon Landsborough. Yes, it had had pride of place at home when my mother was alive. It sat with Dad's special books, like his first edition of *Four Quartets*, between the fancy carved bookends on the dining-room mantelpiece. After she died it moved from there. I imagine Dad tucking it away somewhere in the big bookshelves. Jack's voice comes back to me: 'He was a bestseller kind of writer, Jen, nothing literary, you know. Went in more for potboilers.' I wonder now if my father was just a tiny bit jealous!

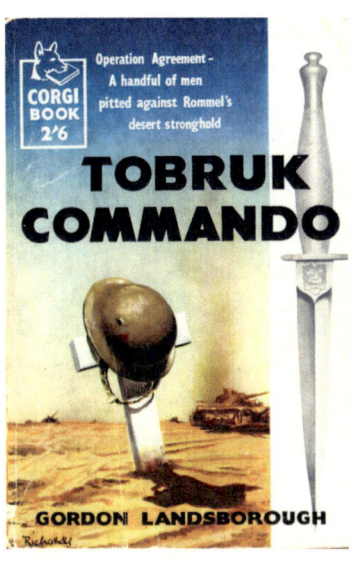

*

Trudie never visited Wanaka. In Queenstown on Christmas Eve 1938 she said goodbye to Bridget, who was going on to relatives in Dunedin, and journeyed northeast towards Omarama and Mount Cook. She travelled by Oldsmobile with a very talkative driver and Mr Stein, a South African German Jew, who was a doctor of music and *most sympathetic and obliging when the twisting twining roads proved to be too much for me and I gave in to car-sickness.* It was a huge relief when they reached the Hermitage, halfway up Mount Cook, and a *hearty welcome awaited us including two men from Bradford who nearly pulled my hand off on hearing I was from Huddersfield and introduced me to everyone as 'Miss Yorkshire' saying that none but a Yorkshire girl would travel alone into the back of beyond to spend Christmas up a bloody high mountain!*

Trudie woke on Christmas morning wondering for a moment where on earth she was. Through the bedroom window she could see the peaks of Mount Cook and Mount Tasman shimmering in the light. She could hardly believe she was going to climb Mount Tasman today, climb on the Tasman Glacier and enter that strange world of ice and snow. She remembered Christmas day a year ago on board the *Oronsay* between Toulon and Naples. It all seemed so very far away now: the Christmas deck games, the splendid dinner and the dance where Jack had partnered her most of the evening and she had begun to think he was quite partial to her. She put the thoughts of Jack from her mind, no point in going there again, and jumped out of bed, determined to really enjoy the expedition.

They climbed high up the glacier in hobnailed boots provided by the hotel. Trudie was frightened at times, glad to be in a good-sized group with experienced climbers, and it was not easy going at all, but totally worth it: the deafening avalanches, the blues and greens reflected in the ice and the dazzling whiteness of the frozen snow. She was relieved at the lunch stop in a small hut. Not exactly an *Oronsay* Christmas dinner but the cold lamb, new potatoes and tinned pineapple tasted brilliant.

That evening, despite the long hike, Trudie was up for the traditional Christmas dinner of turkey and 'Old English plum pudding' and was back on the dance floor waltzing again with the very attractive Scottish lad she'd partnered the night before. But by twelve she 'did a Cinderella' as she had to be up by six and still had packing to do and letters to write. She hurriedly kissed him goodbye and he slipped his address, already written down, into her hand. When she got back to her room she settled down to write home:

Dearest All,
What a thrill it was on Christmas Eve to receive five letters. I didn't notice them on the rack at the Hermitage as I went in but later in the evening, while I was dancing, one of the Bradford-ites brought them along to me. 'Don't you want these Miss Yorkshire?' he said, and if I hadn't been dancing with a VERY nice boy I'm sure I would have dashed off immediately to read them.

She ended the letter with those condolences for the death of William Landsborough. Then her thoughts drifted to Gordon, his son. He was an unusual man, not the run of the mill Huddersfieldian at all. She remembered the crush she'd had on him when they were at school together, despite the fact he was a year or so younger. He was tall for his age, confident and very good-looking. She blushed now as she remembered how she'd follow him home sometimes, hoping he'd turn and see her and talk. Perhaps he always knew she fancied him. She had built fantasies and daydreams around him, imagining him at last realising that she, little Trudie, his second cousin, was really the one for him. But of course nothing had come of it. She had heard that he lived in London now and was making a career as a writer. It must be awful to lose your father, she thought, as her mind drifted on to Dads and his up and down health.

She slept badly that night despite all the fresh air and

exercise. She kept waking up after vivid dreams. She was kissing Gordon Landsborough under that arch in Greenhead Park, but he turned into Gabriel and she didn't understand anything he was saying because she couldn't remember a word of French. Then she was lost up on the glacier and crying for Dads. She woke feeling cold as ice and realised that the heating in the room had gone off and her feet were freezing. Socks! That was what Sandy always said, 'Warm feet means warmth,' so she struggled out of bed and found a thick pair of hiking socks. She lay back in bed concentrating on good memories, good thoughts. She remembered the address she had put away carefully after two nights of dancing and smiled. After all, Edinburgh wasn't so far from Crocketford!

*

I had imagined visiting Mount Cook, or Aoraki to use its Maori name, and the Hermitage, which is still a hotel, when I was rereading the letters and thinking about our trip. It wasn't until I started serious planning that I realised you can't reach Mount Cook from the west side, you can only see it. It was disappointing. I had wanted to visit the place where Trudie had stayed, to walk in her footsteps. And I had liked the idea of the Mauri Aoraki: a peak that reflected the concept of *kaitiakitanga*, a sacred place where the spirits of the ancestors stay. I was perhaps feeling whimsical and imagining Trudie's spirit still there on the glacier.

Instead we pick up the path Jack took on his visit to the west coast six months earlier, sometime in May

1938. He was en route for Auckland, North Island, for his second posting. From Wanaka we crossed the Haast Pass to the wild west coast, driving northwards towards the glaciers, the opposite way to Jack.

I travelled from Christchurch across the Island to the glaciers. The bush scenery down the West Coast was quite unlike anything I have seen. The vegetation is as thick as a tropical jungle. There are huge tree ferns which stand out from the rest of the foliage. The two glaciers. The Fox and the Franz Joseph descend 700 feet to sea level. Right by the ice you have the most luxurious bush. I went out on the ice of the Fox Glacier. I hired equipment and it was good fun scaling the ridges. The crevices though not dangerous are deep and would be nasty to fall into. I crawled through blue ice caves – a blue world. I also took the aeroplane trip. I had a marvellous view of the great peaks and the ice fields below – a magnificent trip though only lasting half an hour.

I reread the letter to Lawrence as we sit on our balcony looking at the peak of Mount Cook, relaxing after our half-hour helicopter trip up the Fox Glacier. No aeroplanes fly now after a series of accidents. We were up at dawn this morning and a little apprehensive. Now we are aglow with excitement and achievement. We know we've been lucky, as the weather is perfect, no clouds and a clear view of the great peaks of Cook and Tasman. We walked on the snow when the helicopter landed, just the two of us alone in a white world. We dissect every moment as we go through the many photographs on the camera, deciding which to keep and which to delete: shots looking up to the glacier, shots of the valley below leading out to Lake Matheson and on to the sea, pictures of the glacier climbers in their equipment, and the photograph the helicopter pilot took of us in the snow looking like an ad for the 'Grey Travellers'. This is my favourite, along with the shots of the trip down, with the white of the ice against the green tropical vegetation. We have fallen in love with this green and white world. I'm pleased to rediscover in the letter that Jack loved it too, and ventured further than us, right into the blue world of the glacier itself. We decide to go back, climb the path on foot that leads you to the mouth of the glacier.

'It doesn't seem too long a walk,' Lawrence decides as he deciphers the little walkers' map we have picked up from the motel. 'We follow the E route to the Chalet Lookout.'

The walk takes us up through woods, climbing quite steeply in parts, crossing dry rivers of stones and rubble where it's difficult to walk. We have to follow the little piles of rocks which mark the way, up and up on difficult terrain.

'I seem to remember from A-level geography this is called terminal moraine.'

Lawrence laughs, as he always does at my attempts to be scientific. He is fascinated by the vegetation, which reminds him of home in the tropical bush and yet is different. 'You could almost be in the Northern Range, but you wouldn't get pines like these, and the smell is different, and those huge tree ferns are like nothing I've seen before.'

At last we come to a little wooden platform that

overlooks the end of the glacier and we can see right up to where we were this morning. There are climbers making their way slowly up the face. They look like peg men from here. I find it difficult to imagine Jack doing that. My Jack, who hardly exercised at all, apart from walking down the road to his local, the Windsor Castle. When I was a little girl I was fascinated by the young Jack that I never knew. I loved looking at the old photographs: Jack as a boy sitting in his back garden with the Miller girls; Jack in whites playing cricket at school, handsome with his dark curly hair; Jack at university taking the part of Faust; and Jack as a young teacher with his pupils at Lyndhurst School. He looked so different from 'Dad', who was bald, plump and a little scruffy in his leather-elbowed sports jacket. I have the same feeling now. A longing to see the young Jack, physically fit, healthily brown, scaling the ridges of the glacier.

We stand together in silence, alone on this little platform below the great glacier. I look around at the strangeness of the landscape and Lawrence echoes my thoughts: 'Yes, a puzzling world here. Look at the tropical vegetation coming right up to the ice. North meets south.'

'It's strange to think of Jack here, in this very place, and Trudie over that peak there, a few months later. What elements of chance brought them finally together to bring me here?'

'What elements of chance led you to me, to bring *me* here?' asks Lawrence.

'It started with that chance meeting at Noel Road, thanks to Pat Hamilton.'

'And was it just chance? In Maori philosophy everything is interrelated: people, objects, past, present and future. There is no such thing as chance. The past is present in the present and the future.'

I think about all the inanimate objects that have brought us here: the letters, the address book, the treasures from the attic, those tokens of the past. Yet most important of all are my memories of Jack and Trudie and what of them is in me, my genetic make-up.

'The Grey Travellers'

CHAPTER 9 – Family Silver

I WAS SIX YEARS OLD and I fell off my bike cycling too quickly down the steep hill of our back lane. The bike jumped into a pothole and threw me right over the handlebars. What a mess! It was the end of the August holidays 1955 and there was no way I could go back to school. I had a black eye, a gap tooth, a cut chin, a bruised shoulder, a cut knee and concussion. My mother was doing home tuition at that time, my brother was at prep school and demanding lots of attention with his bad asthma, and my father, as luck – or bad luck – would have it, was away at a conference. My accident was clearly a problem; I needed looking after. It was Auntie Susie who came to the rescue. Mummy and Peter took me to Bristol on the train and Auntie Susie came up from Newton Abbot to meet me.

I remember that train journey with Auntie Susie vividly. It was the first time I'd spent any time away from my mother, but Auntie made it such fun I didn't shed a tear. As we passed along the Devon coastline and countryside, she named all the interesting places, pointed to the rocks that stood like pillars in the sea, showed me Powderham Castle overlooking the Exe, Dawlish, where the station name was spelled with shells, and Teignmouth, where the sand came close to the rails. As we neared Newton Abbot she explained to me we were going to be staying with my Great-Aunt Marie.

'I'm looking after Auntie Marie in Newton Abbot. She's a little poorly. You must be very nice to her and behave well in her house.'

We got to Auntie Marie's at teatime. A round table was covered with a lace cloth and on the table was silver. I had never seen so much silver, all of it shining so I could see my reflection in it. Silver napkin rings encased their white linen napkins, two silver cake plates of three tiers held a variety of scones, sandwiches and shortcake, a silver tea set stood on its silver tray, a silver tea strainer sat on a silver pot, silver sugar tongs rested in the silver sugar bowl and in the centre of the table a huge silver vase overlooked it all.

I said little during tea, but there was plenty to look at. I imagined I was being a very good girl. I loved my Auntie Susie and didn't want to let her down and I hoped to impress Great-Aunt Marie, for Auntie Susie's sake.

Suddenly Auntie Marie turned to me and said, 'Good God, child, has Gertrude taught you no table manners at all? Look, Susie, at the way she's chewing with her mouth open and holding her knife. We will have to take her in hand.'

And so began my training in being a young lady and learning who I was.

'You have to know how to set a table properly, child. You won't have anyone else to do it for you, not like we did.'

I learned how to put the last-course cutlery next to the mat and work outwards.

'I like the dessert spoon and fork across the top best, shows off the quality of the silver,' Auntie Marie said. 'I don't approve of this modern *French* fad of putting it inside the last-course cutlery.'

She taught me how to clean silver correctly and when Auntie Susie was out at school – she was a teacher like my mother – Auntie Marie would sit me down with a pile of tarnished cutlery to clean.

'One day you'll inherit some of the family silver,' she said. 'I'm sure Gertrude has some'. She showed me the name 'Pearce' on the back of some pieces and the hallmark on others. 'We produced the very best silver,' she said. 'Not just your Great-Uncle Henry of Huddersfield, not just your Great-Grandfather Henry of Huddersfield, but your Great-Great-Grandfather Henry of Grantham and your Great-Great-Great-Grandfather John of Stratford-upon-Avon.'

The day before I was leaving to go home Auntie Marie called me into her bedroom, where I had never been before. In the middle was a huge trunk.

'This is the trunk I take to New Zealand with me,' she said. 'Look, you can read the label. I've heard from your Auntie Susie that you are a good little reader.'

But I couldn't recognise the words; they made no sense whatsoever. She sighed knowingly, as if this proved I was a fraud, not a good little reader at all. Then she sounded out the words carefully: 'Fifty-seven... Bignell Street... Gonville... Wanganui... New Zealand.'

It sounded double Dutch to me. I heard 'Wag a noonie' and imagined it was something to do with a dog.

'This is where your Great-Auntie Win lives,' she continued. 'Her daughter Girlie and her family live nearby. I visit them every three years. I used to go every two years when your Great-Uncle Charlton was alive. Now open the trunk.'

I opened it with dread, half expecting to find a dead Uncle Charlton inside. She pulled out a pale brown soft felt bag. Inside, carefully wrapped in tissue paper, were masses of differently shaped silver spoons. After some thought she chose a small dessertspoon. It was engraved with flowery lines and the handle was moulded into twirls. 'This is for you,' she said. 'You're a good little girl and your table manners are much improved. Look after it carefully. It's very old.'

The spoon, sadly, wasn't looked after carefully and eventually the handle parted from the bowl. Back in North Island, on route to Wanganui, Lawrence and I are talking about which bits of family silver we managed to sell at Christie's, which bits just disappeared and which bits are left. Poor Auntie Marie, what would she have made of life today? Who on earth nowadays wants to clean silver!

'So you have no idea what happened to the New Zealand Pearces?' Lawrence asks.

'None. Who knows? They may still own the house in Bignell Street. Sometimes houses stay in families. I might be about to meet another third cousin, but on the Pearce side. Unlikely to be a match for Stuart Landsborough!'

*

My mother began her last New Zealand letter from Bignell Street on 2 January 1939. She spent a week with her relatives there, after Christmas on Mount Cook. The letter is full of the names of family and friends that would have been familiar to her own family, but mean nothing to me.

I arrived at Wanganui at four pm on December 30th and the sun was shining brilliantly. Auntie Win and Uncle Charlton were there to meet me, and Girlie too. Trudie described the pretty house in Bignell Street, with its broad veranda and the wonderful front garden full of huge chrysanthemums and hydrangeas: *I wish I could bring you some cuttings, Daddy.* At the back there were fruit trees: *passion fruit, peaches, nectarines, and apricots, you would love it here, Dads.*

I do know from the many references in the letters that my grandmother and my Uncle Henry came to Australia and New Zealand perhaps a year before my mother's visit. But not my grandfather, 'Dads'. One of the family mysteries for me is how Gertrude Pearce, Mumsie, from the middle-class conventional jeweller's family, married Thomas Landsborough, the credit draper from Scotland, whose ancestors were labourers and small tenant farmers. She was a staunch teetotaller who always wore a little white ribbon. He loved his whisky. She was quiet and demure and he was expansive and garrulous. I have no idea how they met. I do know they married in 1903, when she was thirty-one and he was twenty-seven. Even as an old man with poor sight and a gammy leg he cut a handsome figure. Was it a grand passion that led Gertrude away from a more 'respectable' marriage, or was she feeling 'on the shelf' and the courtship by this young draper who quoted Robbie Burns and had dreams of grandness led her into thinking he too could be successful in business like her father and brothers? What did the Pearce family think? Was she putting them all to shame? I have the impression that Auntie Marie, certainly, did not approve.

*

We stop at a large supermarket to load up with provisions for our stay in the remote Riverside Lodge on the Whanganui River. At the checkout I ask directions to Bignell Street, Gonville. The person serving hasn't a clue where it is, so she finds a colleague who knows Gonville. We are given complex directions. It seems to be a suburb a little way out. I had imagined it as central. I had seen a leafy broad street by the river, with Auntie Marie arriving at an elegant house a little like the one in Newton Abbot. She draws up in a limousine that she's hired at the railway station. 'I'm exhausted,' she announces. 'Six weeks at sea, a train journey from Wellington, and no one to meet me at the station!'

We set off on our hunt and drive up a long hill into suburban streets. Soon we are totally lost. Eventually we stop and I ask for directions again from a passer-by. 'Do you know Bignell Street in Gonville?'

'Are you sure that's where you want?' he says.

'Yes.' I repeat the address.

He directs me, then adds, 'Careful now, it's a bit rough there, especially the far end of the street.'

As we turn into Bignell Street we wonder at the man's caution. It seems just an ordinary suburban street, but as we drive further down towards 57 we begin to see what he means. Some houses are boarded up and weeds grow high in gardens. There is litter in the street. We pull up slowly at 57. It is brightly painted in purples and greens. We can hardly see the house itself, for in what was once the front garden is a huge trailer painted in matching purple and green. There is a tree in the middle of the garden that has gone wild and blocks the view of the house itself. What might once have been a cultivated lawn, and flowerbeds with chrysanthemums, has disappeared under a sea of junk.

'You might as well take some photographs,' Lawrence says.

'I'm not sure I want to intrude.'

I worry that the residents might think I'm taking pictures for sinister reasons, maybe to report them for antisocial behaviour. But, as we've got here at last, I decide to take a couple. I get out and begin to snap. Suddenly I'm aware of someone in the next-door garden. I look up and see an enormous guy. He's Maori and is marked all over in the most amazing tattoos. I don't want to stare.

'I hope I'm not disturbing anyone,' I say nervously.

'No!' he says and laughs. 'You can't disturb those weirdos next door.'

'I'm taking photos of the house that my relatives once owned.'

'Go on, go on. No one will mind. They come and go there, plenty of different people since we've been here... I bet it was different when your folks were here!'

'Oh, that was over fifty years ago, at least.'

'You see,' he continues, 'they work a system here. Once the likes of us move in the value goes down, then after a bit the property developers come back, buy it all up for a song and make it posh again.'

The story is familiar. I think of Rachman in Notting Hill in the 1950s. A place goes down, you buy it up cheap, let it to poor people, or migrants, or new arrivals, forcing the price lower, then you start to raise the rents and squeeze people out. Eventually you sell it for a fortune.

Yet I had heard that the Maoris had received good reparation for their lands. I wonder why they are still being exploited. I ask him about this.

'Yes, some of us are lucky. Some get crown lands and make a mint from tourism, but some of us don't. My ancestors were pushed into King Country. One of them is said to have been a Maori king. Although it's called that after our kings, the land was poor, no good for a king or a pauper. Eventually my family moved on to this city for work. Me, I am working damn hard to get my family out of here to a nice place where the schools are good. I want my kids to succeed, go to university. Not like that lot next door.'

We both turn to look at the sad state of 57. Poor Auntie Marie I think, and I smile. He smiles too.

'Enjoy your holiday,' he says, 'and take as many pictures as you like.' He turns back into the house.

'Thank you!' I call. 'Thanks for *your* family history.'

It's a blue sunny day and although we have a longish drive ahead we decide to visit Kai Iwi beach, just north of Wanganui, where Trudie went on New Year's day 1939.

On Sunday, New Years Day, we went to Kai Iwi Beach to see Girlie's family. It was a beautiful day, the first they'd had for a week. Girlie and Jim wanted to show me the way the coastline is being eroded so we set off along the beach jumping over the high waves but on the way back the tide had suddenly come in and Jim had to carry us around the point, one at a time, a good job he's strong as Girlie is no light weight! Then we bathed in the sea at the little beach. The waves were strong but it was exhilarating! My first bathe since leaving Albany.

Isn't Ray a lovely youngster? He and I were soon great cobbers and he was quite ready to pack his bag and come to England with me. The day was far too short but I really felt as if I'd known Jim and Girlie all my life and little Ray all his.

The beach is unspoiled. It's a small bay and very quiet. The sea is calm and blue, no rolling waves like Trudie had, although it is a similar time of year. Behind the beach are mobile homes and a small café where we can sit outside and watch the sea.

'I wonder what happened to the Pearce family here?' I say to Lawrence. 'If Girlie was the only surviving child of Winnie and Charlton, the name Pearce would have gone. And they certainly wouldn't be living here now.'

'The child Ray could still be alive. How old would he be? Around eighty? But you don't know the name.'

'No. I checked the family tree but couldn't find a *Girlie*, *Jim* or *Ray*. But it's not them who really interest me, I could have researched on ancestry.co.uk if I was serious. It's not family history I'm searching for. It's my own family: Jack and Trudie.'

'And are you finding them?' Lawrence asks gently.

'Not in the actual houses: 57 Bignell Street, 4 Vaucluse Street or Jack's Glencairn Street. Houses themselves change as their inhabitants come and go.'

'I love visiting my old houses, as you know, even though they have dilapidated, changed, or whatever.'

We laugh. We have gone often, in Trinidad, to the houses where Lawrence grew up. I have named it 'the bore tour'. But those houses are fertile, they yield memory. I remember driving past my old house on the Mount, though it gave me the heebie-jeebies. The front garden with its neat lawn and cut hedges bears no resemblance to my garden, the old blue wooden gate long gone, but I still remember what went on inside.

'No. Here it's not the houses. It's seeing the landscapes, the flora and fauna, through my parents' eyes. Hearing their voices in the letters. Finding small remnants of their lives: the photographs of and by Mr de Neve, Albany with the RM's house, the picture of the Bourgainville and Cosmo's café.'

'And for Jack,' Lawrence adds, 'the articles about his friends in Dunedin, imagining him up on the glacier in his climbing gear, like those climbers we saw, and the beauty of Lake Manapouri, the lake of his 'sorrowing heart.'

We fill up with petrol before we leave for the Whanganui River road. It's a long road with no petrol stations on it. It's described by the Lonely Planet as 'one of the most picturesque drives in the whole of North Island. The native bush here is thick podocarp broad-leaved forest interspersed with fern.' We will follow it to its northernmost end, where we'll join the main road sixty kilometres south of Taumarunui. We are off on an adventure into the unknown, first stop Riverside Lodge.

I discovered Riverside Lodge in the Lonely Planet, not on the internet. The description appealed: 'An isolated converted farm house up the Whanganui river in idyllic surroundings. It's for those who love quiet, all you will hear are the cries of birds, the whispering wind and the river running through.'

In my imagination I saw a tropical landscape. A long lonely river covered by tall trees and thick undergrowth. I must have been half remembering our trip up a tributary of the Demerara River, Kamuni Creek, in Guyana. Here we travelled by boat to stay in the remote Arrowpoint Lodge, run by the indigenous Amerindians. North Island New Zealand landscape is nothing like that. The Whanganui River runs through a deep valley surrounded by rolling hills covered in sheep. It is closer to the landscape I grew up in, in Shropshire, although it is even less inhabited and far more expansive. The single-track road hugs the river. There are no villages and few houses along the first section. Eventually we reach the farmhouse, where we pick up the key for our lodgings. Our hosts are very friendly but happy to let us just get on with it. A mile further up we find it: a secluded house in a flowering garden, with balconies at front and back. Everything in the house is clearly labelled. There are little notes to explain gadgets and make us feel welcome. A picnic breakfast is left in a basket. It is perfection!

Lawrence sniffs out every corner of the house and comments on every view. He quickly finds a perfect little desk in the corner of the living room which he commandeers, his notebooks placed as if they belong already.

We take a stroll along the river. It's warm and balmy and there are no human sounds apart from shouts from an occasional boat. Sheep bleats and birdsong fill the air. The river is so inviting that we strip off our clothes and plunge in naked, forgetting just how cold it's likely to be. Not like our warm swim in Kamuni Creek, Guyana, where the giant hummingbirds flashed past us on iridescent wings. Later, on our balcony, we drink champagne and picnic on the goodies we bought in Wanganui, as dusk turns to night. As we eat and drink we discuss the project.

'I feel I've really got to know the young Trudie. Her letter from Bignell Street says it all. She's so affectionate, enjoys people so much, is thrilled to meet her family here, but also warmly concerned about those back home... all the messages for Susie and Henry and Alec and Kathleen. But Jack... young Jack, he's still a bit of a mystery.'

'Yes, but not 'old Jack'. I remember him vividly,' Lawrence says, 'despite only knowing him such a short time.' He recalls the time Jack stayed with us at Noel Road soon after we'd met. How he was so unfazed by our relationship, so open to Lawrence. 'And,' Lawrence continues, 'that first visit to the flat in Tottenham. Yes, Jack as I remember him, sitting among his books and papers. I could see his need for you. I could see what had been a long companionship since your mother's death.'

I also remember it clearly, the kind of talk we would have on those visits: some article in the *Guardian*, some news of the Labour Party and possibly what Roy Jenkins or Denis Healy was saying on a matter of home policy or the economy of the day. Our youthful radical convictions sometimes clashing with his more moderate take on things. This was Jack, in his mid-sixties, thoughtful, compassionate and interested in our lives and our views.

How different from that young man whose head is filled with the romance of landscape, with passionate desires that are unfulfilled, with radical ideas and a strong need to prove himself. But prove himself to whom? To the world, to his father or to Joyce?

'It's strange,' I say, 'to think that you, so fit and healthy, are older now than Jack was when he died.'

We remember that family Christmas in Shrewsbury when we'd all gone back to stay in Auntie Philippa's house: Dad, me, Peter and Lawrence, the new boyfriend. We had tried hard to make Christmas Day work. I think we all knew it would be the last, but Peter had gone on a drinking binge to escape from the grief he felt over Jack, and Dad was full of anxieties about his own failing health and about the failures of his son.

'I remember him telling me, one evening when I'd gone to say goodnight, how glad he was that I'd met you. I think he had already realised that he didn't have long.'

Later, as night thickens and it gets too cold to sit out, we move in. In the far corner of the living room we discover some records and an old-fashioned record player. All our favourite oldies are here. We smooch to Simon and Garfunkel's 'Bridge Over Troubled Water' and Rod Stewart's 'Maggie May', remembering our own young love, stimulated by our conversation and these melodies from the early 1970s. What a contrast to the late 1930s and to my parents' love. There is Trudie smitten by Jack but with no response coming. As she spends her last few nights in New Zealand with the Pearce family at Wanganui she has no idea that he's been just fifty miles north at New Plymouth. She imagines him on the *Oronsay* halfway across the Pacific.

CHAPTER 10 – No Name

YOU CAN GET TO TAUMARUNUI
Going north or going south
And you pull in there at midnight
and there's cinders in your mouth
You got cinders in your whiskers
and a cinder in your eye
So you hop off for refreshments
for a cup of tea and pie
In Taumarunui, Taumarunui,
Taumarunui on the main trunk line.

'Taumarunui on the main trunk line'

As we drive into Taumarunui I'm singing the old folksong. It is such a pity that I can't sing well. I'm like both my father and my mother in that way. Dad always used to mumble bits of songs, like this one, a few lines, then a strange humming sound. Lawrence too only knows a chorus, but at least he has a voice. We sing bits of songs as we drive, especially if we're feeling tired, like today, after the twisting drive along the Whanganui River. I give him the words as he sings the tune. This old car from Omega has no CD or tape player. The song is about a railway man who falls in love with a yellow-haired girl who serves him tea and pie. As we park I search through the file for the right letter, the one from Taumaruni on the main trunk line.

Jack wrote to his parents from here on 20 October 1938:

Actually, at the moment I'm in the waiting room at Taumarunui Station. I've been on a short observation trip into one of the wildest and most forgotten parts of New Zealand right in the heart of the country, Kings' Country, it's called after the Maori kings. The official reason for my visit is the observation of schools, but actually I've had plenty of time to see the country. It's the part of North Island east of Taranaki and west of the central mountains. I got into Tamuruni here at 7o'clock, went to the pictures, had supper in the only hotel. And I am now awaiting the mid-night express back to New Plymouth.

The old station is now, in 2011, the tiny tourist office, or i-SITE, as they call it here. The woman behind the counter is excited when she reads my letter; it must be a change from her normal routine. 'You'll find the hotel and the cinema almost exactly as they were then, at least on the outside.' She hurries to the door and points down the main road, Hakiaha Street, to the old hotel where Jack had his supper. Beyond we can see the cinema, looking as if it hasn't been renovated since his visit. On the wall of the tourist office is a large painting of the railway station as it was in 1938, full of passenger and freight trains, customers arriving and departing, and the famous 'refreshments for a cup of tea and pie'.

Here, in forgotten Taumarunui, this once great railway Mecca, even the freight trains don't stop. No need for a railway station, and not much need for a tourist office either. The Lonely Planet has written it off completely: 'Maybe Taumarunui should get a gimmick, as this little town can feel a bit grim.' We discover that the Lonely Planet, our reliable guide, is wrong. The enthusiastic tourist officer gives us a brochure which describes 'The Forgotten World Highway which offers an unparalleled journey through our pioneering and Maori past in the richest of landscapes'. We also note that '12km of the Forgotten World Highway is unsealed road. There are no petrol stations along the whole 150km road which follows the ancient Maori trade routes and pioneering farm tracks.' So, after filling the tank and buying bottles of water, we enter this wild and forgotten part of New Zealand: King Country. This must be the area where the ancestors of the Wanganui Maori of Bignell Street came from.

Much of our route follows the old railway line towards Stratford and New Plymouth, Jack's actual journey:

It consists of ranges and ranges of hills, much which is clad in virgin bush, although a great deal has old tree stumps and secondary growth. Much of the land belongs to the Maoris. When they were driven out of Waikato they retreated south to this far less hospitable landscape. Yet another example of colonial injustice.

In 1995, according to the guide, the Waikato tribes received a full crown apology with the return of some of the land and some compensation for the rest. A pity Dad never knew this.

'If only I could tell him about our trip,' I say to Lawrence. 'To travel in time...'

'Look! We are back in time.' Lawrence points to the old railway bridge that spans the valley, once the main way of travelling across the Island.

'If only I had asked him more...'

As we drive through the Tangarakau Gorge, through the magnificent podocarp forest, I reread Jack's description: *The bush comes right down to the track, at times you wonder if the train will make it.* He's dozing through the night, waking in the early light to this landscape. Was he thinking about his work? Was he excited by the scenery in the way we are? Was he homesick for London, Dulwich, his mum and dad? Joyce? Did he spare a thought for Trudie Landsborough and wonder what she was up to?

We stop in the Republic of Whangamomona for lunch. It was once a busy frontier town of pioneers: 300 inhabitants, according to the plaque. Now there are fifty. In 1989 it became a self-declared republic, the residents, who were angry at losing their township status, were even more furious at being left off the map. The old Whangamomona hotel serves a good lunch and we are the only visitors.

We spread Jack's letters out on the table, the New Plymouth letters, and discuss our plans for tracking him. Lawrence, still intrigued by Jack's thoughts on Germany and the approaching war, reads from the first letter, dated 28 September 1938.

Dear Mum and Dad,
These are unsettled times indeed. I was waiting for some definite news from Europe but the turmoil is still going on; we can only hope for the best. I am speaking on Germany this Friday to the Taranaki teachers. I shall go on appealing for sympathy with them as an oppressed people and I shall say that war if it comes must be a war against Fascism alone.

'I think we should check in the old newspapers again,' he suggests, 'see if there's a report. Look, there's a little pencil note here, on the next letter home, saying *see cutting.*'

I squint at the note, very faint as we've photocopied from the original letters, which have been left safe back at home. I can just read it. We never found the article referred to in the Dunedin letter, despite Lawrence's arduous hunt through microfilm in the library.

'We can try,' I say, 'but remember how tricky it is when archives aren't digital.'

I flick through another letter.

'He's very delighted with New Plymouth. *It seems queer to think of Europe so troubled and this place so beautiful, so perfect, so sunny. Of all the places I've lived in New Zealand I think New Plymouth the best.* These letters sound so enthusiastic compared to the others. He seems more relaxed, much happier, more open.'

We are enjoying the fun of analysing each word, each possible clue to Jack's life. He is often quite formal and guarded in his letters home; they are constructed to make him seem a very serious young man, intellectual, thoughtful. Of course he hopes to be a writer. He very much has his parents in mind as he writes, especially his father, whom he was terribly anxious to please. A stern man, from what he told me, unlike Grannie Annie, who was warm and loving and, as I remember her, full of life and fun.

After our late lunch in the hot afternoon we drive on and on. At last Mount Taranaki appears in the distance, with its snow-clad peak glimmering in the sun. Jack loved it: *the most perfect mountain in the world.* We stop so I can photograph the peak, then I take over the driving. We are both really tired. It's been a fantastic day's journey, but we've been on the move for nearly twelve hours and even the singing doesn't seem to work. As we enter Stratford, I know we're on our last lap. Then I notice someone flashing me from behind. It's a police car. I pull over, feeling panic building. Lawrence wakes up from his doze, bemused.

'Madam, do you realise you've been driving at fifty miles an hour through a built-up area?'

'No', I say. 'I had no idea. I'm not fully used to the New Zealand road signs and it doesn't seem very built up.'

He looks at me hard and I can see him thinking,

'Where is this English lady coming from?'

'I think you'd better let your husband drive you on to New Plymouth.'

Back on our journey, with Lawrence now at the wheel, we relish the policeman's kindness. We have heard about the enormous fines you can pay in New Zealand for driving offences. He was old-fashioned, perhaps, in his view of a woman driver, but what a stroke of luck to get an avuncular policeman. How awful it would have been on this last lap of our trip round New Zealand to get a large fine or even a summons for 'dangerous driving'.

We are lucky in New Plymouth too. The pretty Cottage Mews, which I booked online some months ago, is easy to find and it turns out to be right round the corner from the Central School, where Jack taught, and from Liardet Street, where he boarded at Marsland View:

I found a very nice place to stay, the best I've struck yet. It's slightly more expensive but well worth it; as a permanent I'm allowed to use the private sitting room of the family and am in fact quite welcomed as one of the family. The children and staff of the school are grand. The school is only two minutes walk from my lodgings.

This evening, sitting out on our little balcony relaxing after our long day, I go back to the letters again and read out some key lines:

I'm well and very happy. As you know I have many dear friends in New Plymouth. I'm having a lovely time here in

New Plymouth, if people planted a town according to their heart's desire it could not be much more beautiful.

'Their heart's desire? That is strong language!'

'Perhaps,' suggests Lawrence, 'he's in love.'

'Of course! That's it! This must be where he met the woman... the woman in the photograph. I'd always imagined it was Auckland, as he spent longest there, but it must have been here.'

I start rummaging through all my papers for the photograph. I'm sure I brought it with me. It's not in with the file of letters. I search through the travel documents and it's not there either. Totally exhausted, I can't face unpacking completely. I decide to leave it until the morning.

It's been a mammoth drive from Riverside Lodge, right up the Whanganui River, on to Taumarunui, then the 'Forgotten World Highway', which did indeed take us back into the past. We have crossed to this far west point of North Island. We've almost done a circle. Yet, as I lie in bed, I can't sleep. I'm overtired. I keep thinking about the photograph. I hate losing precious things; I've lost so many.

*

In June 1974 I made the last trip to the home of my childhood at 111 The Mount, to do the final sorting.

As the train pulled in I saw my father waving. I recall, now, how struck I was at that moment by how thin he had grown. He was slightly stooped, not the well-built man I had lived my life with. Anxiety, love, grief welled up, but I firmly pushed my emotions away and stepped out of the train, smiling, to meet him.

'I've done a bit more sorting,' was the first thing he said.

Sorting the three-storey Victorian house was a challenge. I had spent every day of my Easter holiday on it, while he had been in hospital. Then every day of the half-term break. Dad had done a little, but he just wasn't strong enough to manage the physical work, and he had found the sorting of his papers difficult, what to keep and what to throw away. He had never been good at chucking. Very little had been organised over the fifteen years since my mother's death. There were still odd remnants of her things and of Grannie Annie's. Newspapers were stacked in piles: *Guardians*, *New Statesmans*, *British Psychological Journals*, *Ethical Records*. Piles of opened post littered every surface. I had thrown away a lot but little mounds were still there for Dad to make the final decisions on: what he would take to his new, small flat near me in London and what would have to go.

'I've still got the box room to do,' I told him. 'It's the last big job.' I had an afternoon and a morning to get it done. I knew I neeeded to be ruthless. I did want to be back in London early – I was hoping for a phone call from the boy I'd just met. 'Just leave me to it,' I said. 'If I'm unsure about anything I'll check with you.'

The box room was at the top of the attic stairs between the two large bedrooms. It had a sloping ceiling so you could only stand at one end. It was crammed with old cases, cardboard boxes, trunks and an old hatbox. Although I knew I had to be quick and determined, I felt that I couldn't just let my parents' lives slip through my fingers into the bin. I decided to keep any personal letters and any photographs that showed people I knew. The damp and must tickled my nose as I opened the first case. It was full of tiny brown and white snaps. I didn't recognise the people or the places, apart from one of my father lying out in some woods, smoking a pipe. There was a camp kettle boiling. The trees looked strange, very tall. I decided it must be from his time in New Zealand. I added it to the 'yes' pile' and threw away the rest in a sudden 'what the hell?' decision. Remembering it all now, I feel like screaming! What photographs, what records of his life here in New Zealand, in New Plymouth, did I throw away?

Many boxes were full of Dad's old academic papers on psychology; they went too. There were essays written in German from his time at King's. I chucked those, but picked out the photo which was among them, Dad playing Faust.

By the end of the Sunday morning, when my time was running out, I reached the very end of the room, where I had to crawl to reach the containers. I came across an oddly shaped box. It was wooden and, I discovered, opened to form a desk top with a green baize covering. There was a thin drawer at the bottom and I dug my fingers into it, really squeezing them in. They touched what felt like an envelope. I pulled hard. Out came a small mottled brown cardboard case with a flap tucked into a slit. Inside, stuck to the cardboard backing, was a brown and white photograph of a beautiful young woman. She looked like an old movie star, yet her dress was not glamorous, she was not adorned with earrings or pearls. Her brown hair was wavy and parted in the middle. Her dress was of dark fabric with a modest V neckline. Her eyes, her nose and her smile were beautiful. I didn't recognise her at all. It certainly wasn't one of my aunts. I thought of Joyce, but this was not at all how I imagined her, not how Dad had described her. Joyce, he had said, was 'tall, blonde and athletic'.

I went downstairs with the photograph. 'Who on earth is this?' I asked. My father looked up from his pile of papers and peered into the picture. Then he stood up and took it from me gently. He looked at it silently for what had seemed a long time. Then he quietly said her name.

'Who is she?' I asked.

'She was the girl I fell in love with in New Zealand. She broke my heart,' he said simply.

I had thought, back then, that I knew everything about my father's life. I was shocked.

'I fell for her completely and she for me. We even got engaged. Yet in the end she wouldn't leave, too difficult for her to come. There was the war looming, of course.'

'Did you keep in touch?'

'No. She married her old boyfriend soon after. Never mind. So long ago now.' He sighed and looked up from the photograph, then smiled. 'And anyway, you wouldn't be here now, would you?'

I was surprised at the powerful hug, even though he was frail. It was quite unusual for him. I took back the photograph from him. Before I returned to my work in the box room I popped it into my bag. I wonder, now, why he let me keep it.

*

As I wake this morning I remember exactly where it is. I had packed it in the zipped inner pocket of my hand luggage, putting it there so it wouldn't get crushed or creased.

'Here she is! I've found her.' I show the photograph to Lawrence, although he has seen it before. 'I just wish I could remember her name.'

'Are you sure Jack told you?'

'Definitely. I think it might have begun with M.'

'Marjorie? Maureen? Megan? Miriam? Muriel?' Lawrence pauses, trying to find yet another girl's name typical of that generation. 'Maggie May!' he jokes.

It's Sunday and the library is shut. We take photographs of the school and walk up and down Liardet Street looking for Marsland View. One elegant house fits the description, with its view of Marsland Hill from the back garden. It is exactly two minutes from the school and it looks large enough to have been a small hotel. Lawrence decides to ask. I'm never keen to disturb people but I do watch excitedly as he walks up the driveway and knocks. There's quite a long conversation. I start imagining that relatives of the owners still live here. However, I can tell, as I watch him return, that we've not been lucky. The owner was friendly, I learn, and, like everyone we have told our story to, was eager to help, but he had no idea of the history of the house; who had lived there, what it had been.

Just beyond, at the top of Liardet Street, is the entrance to Pukekura Park, with the iconic view of

Mount Taranaki, or Mount Egmont as it was in Jack's time. We walk in past the cricket pitch and find the water garden with its little café, a good place to pause and read. Here are where the views are best, according to Jack:

Pukekura Park is said to be the most beautiful park in New Zealand – full of wonderful tree ferns and native flora; there's a lovely ornamental water garden across which, ten miles distant towering to the skies rises the mighty peak of Egmont, 8000ft above the sea, probably the most perfect mountain in the world. It's covered with snow and when the sun pours down upon the upper slopes it transforms them into a cone of dazzling white.

Pukekura Park and Mount Taranaki (Jack's Egmont)

As we reread the letter we laugh at his enthusiasm for everything in New Plymouth. 'He's clearly in love,' I say, 'and I'm convinced she's the landlady's daughter as he talks about being *part of the family.*'

Lawrence disagrees. He thinks she's a colleague. 'Not only does he describe the staff as *grand*, he writes: *I've met such nice people here. I've an open invitation from one member of staff and I'm welcome in their home whenever I feel like strolling round.* He's probably referring to her but doesn't want to be explicit to his parents. Who is the *we* he refers to when he goes after school for *a dash in the surf and a sunbathe?*'

Opposite the garden there's a little path half hidden by bush. We climb up a small slope and find a bench among the red-flowered 'Christmas bushes', the pohutukawa, and the tree ferns. Though partly enclosed, it has a perfect view of the water garden and the mountain beyond.

'This is where they would sit,' I say, as if it's a fact, not our fiction.

We sit there quietly, comfortable in our own silence. I think of Jack, that young man I never knew, with his beautiful girl. He's convinced that he is in love, deeply enough to try and persuade her to come back with him to Europe. Of course he didn't know then that very soon London would be bombed.

And what is she thinking? Feeling? Is she charmed by this romance with the handsome young teacher from Britain? He quotes poetry and refers to novels by European writers. He writes himself and sends his articles back to a magazine in England to be published. He talks politics. He loves Germany but condemns the National Socialists. If he wasn't asthmatic he would have fought against Franco. He conjures for her his life in London and tries to convince her she'll be happy there. His parents will love her, he assures her, his mother is a most open and generous person, full of fun and humour; his father is a little more stiff, but a good principled man. Dulwich is a quiet part of London. No, the park is nothing like as beautiful as this; but there's an art gallery and a museum. London itself has its theatres, concert halls and galleries. London is the centre of the world.

And is she tempted? She's never met anyone like Jack. She heard him lecture on Germany to an audience of a hundred people. He's so confident and assured. Her life has been this small town. The young man she was seeing before Jack arrived is a good man but she's known him all her life. She's only known Jack for two months. It's been a whirlwind romance, and he has to leave New Zealand soon. How can she leave with him? Impossible. She couldn't hurt her parents and suddenly leave her whole life behind. Yet she could follow later... maybe? She understands now what is meant by 'falling' in love. She's fallen from a dizzy height. She's fallen from the top of Mount Egmont. How will she survive?

This evening, after we've seen the festival of lights illuminating Pukekura and listened to the music of the local bands, we sit again on our balcony to discuss our day, relishing these warm nights. Our talk returns to Jack.

'Listen to this from his 24 October letter: *I'm afraid I've kept you waiting rather a long time for a letter.* He's just too in love to write.' I laugh.

'Look, there's more here on Germany.' Lawrence reads: '*The international situation still looks pretty sticky.*

I'm afraid the cost of Peace is going to be heavy. If Germany succeeds in putting a wedge between France and Russia things will look pretty bad. Fascism's blackmail will certainly have triumphed then. Do you think he was serious about asking her to go back with him? It would have been so difficult for her, especially at that time.'

'I wonder. Perhaps they really were desperately in love. If only I'd asked Dad more, when I had the chance. I had intended to, but, as you know, it all happened so quickly.' We sit quietly remembering those last few months of his life, the first few months of us. 'It's a coincidence that I discovered the photograph just two days after I first met you.'

'It's all a coincidence. The fact I went to the party in the first place.'

I had thrown a midsummer party. I had invited all the young men that I had a fancy for, as I wanted to cure a broken heart. I had gone to the West End, to the hairdressers, and had changed my style to curly and gypsy. I had bought a white frilly lace blouse to match my red Laura Ashley skirt. But none of the young men had come. I had been standing in the basement kitchen, pouring drinks for my guests, feeling a little flat, when I looked up towards the open stairwell. I had seen, to my surprise, a stranger, an uninvited guest. He was a beautiful boy: very dark, a lovely smile. I thought to myself, 'He'll do!' At twenty-four I already knew that love rarely ran smoothly. You wanted what you couldn't have, and when you had it you didn't want it. I was flattered as I registered his interest in me, that lovely smile.

'We smooched to "Maggie May" all evening,'

Lawrence says.

I laugh. We've recalled this moment so often it might not even be true. It's a memory of a memory.

'It was waking up in that little room of mine, above the canal, and wondering what on earth I was doing with this strange man in my bed that I remember most clearly, then realising I had to be catching a train home in an hour.'

'And I saw you off on the train at Euston and promised to phone you on Sunday evening. What if I hadn't decided to tag along with Pat and David to the party?'

*

The following morning, our last in New Plymouth, we get to the library early, just as it opens. I want to find some record of Marsland View. It was a hotel *registered with the Government Tourist Bureau* so it should be possible. I'm hoping to discover who the landlady was and who her family were. Was there a grown-up daughter? I also want to check any records of the Central School, see if Jack's name is actually there. Lawrence will check the old newspapers again for records of the talks Jack gave on Germany at New Plymouth, Stratford and Opunake. He is now the expert on the microfilm machine.

We meet another amazing librarian, Suzanne. She seems as determined as we are to find evidence of Jack. In the *New Plymouth Streets Directory 1938* she finds Mrs Anne Liston listed as owner of the Marsland View Hotel. It was number 74 then and is where Leach Street crosses Liardet. There is no mention of the family. Apparently the building has long gone, the site a warehouse now, Suzanne tells us sadly.

Lawrence is having no more luck here ploughing through the local newspapers of October 1938 than he did in Dunedin. Clearly the talks on Germany were not of local importance; the cutting sent home to Dulwich could have been from an educational journal. Time is ticking on and we need to get going on our journey back to Auckland. We are packing up to leave when Suzanne returns from her hunting looking very pleased.

'I discovered this in the education yearbook for Central School,' she says excitedly. 'It's a photograph taken in 1939 of all the staff who taught there between 1930 and 1939. Maybe your father is there. It's a reunion photograph.'

I look hurriedly for Jack, then realise he can't be there as he left at Christmas 1938:

It was a nice breaking up time. I acted as Father Christmas to the infant department and it was a great success. It was my job to distribute presents among the little ones, and to make a fuss of them generally. And so the stay in New Plymouth is over. It was with a huge wrench that I left there – Goodbye Mountain, goodbye lovely gardens, goodbye dear friends.

Then I reach in my file for the photograph of the *dear friend*. I undo the little brown flap and open it up. I look at her and then along the rows of faces.

'There she is!' I shout, disturbing the quiet of the library.

'No Name'

Lawrence rushes up and Suzanne looks over my shoulder.

'There! She's right in the middle of the front row, just above the label 1930–1939'.

They both peer into the photograph. She sits neatly, knees together, hands folded. She's wearing a white dress and white hat and gloves, quite striking against her tan. She's very pretty; you can see that here even though the photograph is small. There's no wistful or lovelorn look on her face! She is beaming at the camera.

Suzanne looks back at the original photograph. 'Yes,'

she agrees, 'it's definitely her. You can tell by the smile.' She is as excited as we are. 'Maybe you could check the records at the education department?' she suggests. 'They may have lists of names.'

We haven't the time and also, unless everyone in the photograph was listed in order, how would we match Jack's 'dear friend' to a name?

'We'll just have to call her "No Name",' I say, as we drive out of beautiful New Plymouth on the final stage of our route back to Auckland. Together, we start singing:

'Maggie I couldn't have tried any more...
You lured me away from home
Just to stop you from being alone
You stole my heart
And that's what really hurts...'

'Who stole whose heart?' I ask, interrupting our song. 'Was it the girl in the photograph or Jack? And what about poor Trudie? If anyone's heart was stolen, it must surely have been hers!'

CHAPTER 11 – Harbours

Jack sat on the small beach at Castor Bay under the shade of a pohutukawa tree, which was still in bloom with its red 'Christmas' flowers. He was supposed to be writing to his parents but instead he was daydreaming as he stared out at the Hauraki Gulf. It was exactly ten days since he'd seen her. She had made it clear in the end that she would not come, but he had still held out hope. Tomorrow he was leaving on the *Monterey*, saying goodbye to New Zealand and her, perhaps for ever. Maybe she'll come and see me off, he mused. She had told him she couldn't bear to do that... wave a handkerchief at a departing boat, yet he so longed to see her again. He hoped against hope that she would be there, even if just to say goodbye once more... to hold her again, to kiss her. Jack sighed. He must get on with this letter home.

Castor Bay, Near Auckland

8/1/39

Dear Mum and Dad,
I was glad to get all the Xmas news. This I'm afraid must be a rushed letter, just a few lines. I set sail tomorrow and arrive at Honlolulu on the 18th after calling at Suva and Pago Pago. I've had a quiet time since I left New Plymouth. I'm staying at my friends the Boxes. They have a lovely

summer bungalow overlooking the Hauraki Gulf with all its beautiful islands. The sea is calm and warm and blue. I shall be so sorry to leave tomorrow.

Jack paused and looked up and out to sea. He could hardly believe that he was really leaving. There had been times, before New Plymouth, when he had longed for the year to end... but not now. He forced his mind away from her and squinted as he looked towards where Auckland was, trying to make out the skyline. Tomorrow he would get up early and catch the first train in. He'd have a last look round that lovely city. His luggage was already deposited; he just had his overnight bag. He'd revisit Symonds Street, walk across the Domain and on into Parnell. There he'd find a nice little place for lunch before making his way to the port. He would get there in good time, just in case. No! She wouldn't be there, he was just dreaming. He returned to his letter and finished it quickly without expanding on the reasons for his sorrow at leaving New Zealand.

I hope you had a nice Xmas, very cold I heard. Take things easy, both of you, it's not that long before I see you in March. I'll write fully from the boat and post the letter in Suva.
All the very best and love.
Jack

*

I'm having my hair coloured and cut at Raymond's (pronounced the French way) in Parnell. It feels great to be back in Auckland, like we know it already, including where to get our hair cut. The hairdressers is just a walk from our hotel, right opposite the white wooden church of St Mary's in the 'old bit' of Parnell. Lawrence has already had his done; it looks sharp and shows off his dark tan. Now I'm confidently letting Raymond snip away at mine, knowing he cuts like a pro.

'So did you find the block of flats where your father lived off Symonds Street?' he asks. 'Was it where I suggested in Whitaker Place?'

'You had the exact spot, but sadly it had gone. No mansion flats at all, just an empty space.'

'Yes, I'm not surprised. The university has bought most of that land now, right up to the edge of the Domain. There'll be academic blocks or halls of residence there soon.'

I tell him of some of the successes and some of the disappointments in our search across New Zealand. It's exactly a month since we were here at Raymond's the first time.

'Yesterday we drove out to Castor Bay, where my father's friend and colleague Mr Boxer had a summer bungalow overlooking the Hauraki Gulf. What a pretty spot! All those beautiful small volcanic islands.'

'Yes, and a millionaire's paradise.' Raymond sniffs. 'You wouldn't have school teachers owning houses there now. Even somewhere like Ponsonby is really upmarket, with property costing a fortune. Have you eaten there yet? Great restaurants!'

'Yes, we loved it. This evening, our last, we want to eat on the water. Any suggestions?'

Raymond reels off a list of possible places and I note

them down carefully: Euro, Alleluya, Lenin Bar and Barbara's.

It's a perfect summer's night for sitting out by the water watching the boats, all lit up, coming and going from the islands. We haven't gone to one of Raymond's suggestions; instead we find a little fish café on the end of Princes Wharf.

'The *Monterey* may have docked here,' I say to Lawrence as we're sipping our last glass of wine.

'It must have looked quite different then, a big working port, not just pleasure boats and ferries to the islands.'

'Perhaps the big boats docked further up Quay Street, where the commercial port is now?'

'Maybe, but wouldn't they have had to leave via the customs house right here?' Lawrence turns towards the old building. 'This must be roughly the view the passengers had if they were looking back at the city as they set sail.'

'Yes, they would have sailed between the islands of the Hauraki Gulf and on into the ocean.' I look across the dark water trying to imagine it all.

'To the South Pacific.'

'To Pago Pago'.

'I'm sure the "girl-with-no-name" never came to see Jack off,' Lawrence muses, 'never waved goodbye with her handkerchief. Poor Jack! Didn't you say they had actually got engaged but she broke it off at the last minute?'

'That's what I remember from what he told me, but it's years ago now and memory tricks you. She felt she

217

couldn't leave her family and move with him to Europe at such a time. He said, I'm sure, that she ended up marrying her previous boyfriend, the boy from New Plymouth. It's so annoying that I can't even remember her damn name!'

'She must have been very much in your father's mind as he left in early January. It couldn't have been long since they were together. After all he didn't leave New Plymouth till around Christmas or New Year, did he? He talks of being Santa Claus for the kids at his school.'

'Yes. And his last night here was 8 January, according to his letter home.'

*

On 9 January 1939 Trudie climbed up the gangplank of the *Monterey* for her onward journey round the world towards home. The very first person she saw was Jack. She had imagined he had gone on the earlier passage on the *Oronsay*, hurrying back at this difficult time with all the talk of war. Yet here he was, right in front of her. She blushed despite herself. He looked at her and smiled gently in that slightly distracted manner of his.

'Trudie! How very good to see you. I thought you'd be back by now.'

'I thought you would be!'

'I wonder who among the other teachers are on board.'

'Well, Bridget is, I know, but Sandy has gone straight back from Australia.'

'I know Holmes has gone already. Thank God,' he

added, almost to himself.

'Quite so.'

They both laughed conspiratorially.

'I'll see you at dinner,' Jack said, as he went off to find his cabin.

Trudie hoped that they would be on the same table again. She met him strolling on deck before dinner. They exchanged notes about their cabins and what they had seen of the ship.

'I've a big airy cabin and I've noticed beautiful lounges,' Jack remarked. 'It's a better ship than the *Oronsay* but the food has to be tested out. So here's to the *Monterey*!'

Out on deck towards the stern they watched Auckland slip away. Jack was silent, lost in his own thoughts. Trudie wondered if she'd ever see another city with such a beautiful setting. The boat zigzagged through all the tiny islands with their conical shapes: hundreds of extinct volcanoes. The sea was calm as they moved towards the Great Barrier Island and the South Pacific Ocean. It was strange to feel so hopeful in a world that might be about to explode. Yet she was experiencing a strange sense of suspension: Europe and threats of war, home and work, all seemed so far way. There were, after all, two oceans and America to cross. Out on this enormous expanse of blue, she was standing beside the one man she had met whom she thought she could truly love. The future was suddenly irrelevant. It was this very moment that mattered.

*

Our departure is less romantic and less beautiful. We are at the airport waiting for our flight to Rarotonga, the largest of the Cook Islands. No, not Pago Pago, or Pango Pango.

The photograph of the tropical island with the beautiful bay sat on the mantelpiece of my parents' bedroom throughout my childhood. It stayed on the mantelpiece after my mother's death, but whether Dad really noticed it or ever looked at it I have no idea. I have had it since my father died. I keep it in the trunk, Pandora's box, with the rest of my history. It's faded now: the palm trees have yellowed, the sea and sky have paled. Yet it has always represented to me my mother's romantic love for my father in this South Sea isle that she called Pango Pango, the very name sounding mysterious and exotic to my child's ears. I grew up with the desire to go there, to discover for myself the charm of Pango Pango. But I could never find it on a map, or in an atlas, or in an index. Where exactly it was remained a mystery.

Then, when we were living back in Trinidad in 2008, I took some English friends to visit my favourite place right up in the Northern Range, the Asa Wright Nature Reserve. While they did the guided walk into the rainforest I sat on the wonderful old colonial veranda sipping a rum punch and watching the hummingbirds on the feeders flashing their extraordinary colours. Gradually I picked up on the conversation of some serious birders at the next table. One guy was dominating the conversation. He appeared to have been everywhere.

'I've been to every nook of the South Pacific islands

but I've never seen birds like you get here in Trinidad. It's the nearness to South America, to the mainland.'

I leaned over to him and interrupted. 'Have you ever been to a place in the Pacific called Pango Pango?'

He looked at me blankly for a moment and then he said, 'You must mean Pago Pago. It's part of the American Samoan Islands. It is in fact the name of a harbour, although the whole area now is called Pago Pago. It's perhaps the most beautiful harbour I've ever seen. Have you been?'

'No,' I said, 'but I will now.'

And so I had planned to visit Pago Pago when we first seriously discussed the trip to follow in my parents' footsteps across the globe. Then, on 29 September 2009 an offshore earthquake sent a tsunami right into the harbour of Pago Pago, causing serious damage. I saw on television my beautiful harbour destroyed. We could still have gone, but when our travel agent suggested the Cook Islands instead, which we could visit as part of our round the world ticket, it seemed sensible. Travelling to the American Samoan Islands, only a bit further north, would have cost us a fortune to see a harbour no longer the 'most beautiful in the world', no longer the harbour that Jack and Trudie saw in January 1939.

Now, here in Auckland, at the airport, it's 2 February 2011 but we are going to arrive on the the first.

'This is doing my head in,' Lawrence says, as he reads the flight screen for our departure. 'I hate the idea of a day disappearing. Where has it gone to?'

'Nowhere,' I say, and laugh. 'Jack and Trudie would have crossed the international date line on board the *Monterey*. Perhaps they all drank champagne.'

'I don't think we want a glass, do we? Better to have one when we've arrived safely!'

The flight takes only four hours, though minus a day. As we come in to land we both say, 'Tobago.' It's just like arriving at Crown Point, the way the plane descends sharply so you think you're hitting the sea. My first view of the island is like the Tobago I saw back in 1975: a tiny airport, little development, an idyllic tropical island. In so many ways we are going back in time! As we reach Arrivals we are again reminded of the Caribbean. A guy in a straw hat is playing a guitar and singing:

'Oh island in the sun,
Willed to me by my father's hand,
All my days I will sing in praise...'

We can't help but laugh. It seems so strange hearing West Indian calypso here in the South Pacific, where today's 'island tourist culture' has now reached. Then, once through Immigration and Customs, which only takes a few minutes, we are greeted by the reception team for tourism. They robe us with garlands of white frangipani, or *leis*, as they are called here in the South Pacific. Still wearing our garlands while we wait for all the other passengers to arrive on our courtesy bus, we are feeling a bit uncomfortable, but then I'm reminded of something. I rummage in my rucksack and find the photograph that I want.

'Look at this, Lawrence!'

It's a brown and white photo I miraculously still have of Jack and Trudie and two other women, Bridget and Margaret perhaps. They are standing on the deck of a ship. Behind is sea, beach and mountain. Jack is on the left and he looks as if his arm is around Trudie. He is tall, slim and tanned. Still handsome, I think, though his hair is just beginning to recede. He's wearing white trousers gathered at the waist and a loose shirt. He looks trendy, quite modern in fact. It must be the trousers and shirt. Next to him and so much shorter stands Trudie in a checked frock and sandals worn with socks. She looks quite the 'jeune fille' until you peer closely at her face. The two women next to her look older. One is beginning to turn grey, the other wears large-framed spectacles. All of them are garlanded in flowers. Are they looking just a bit self-conscious?

'The South Sea visitors!' Lawrence says, looking at his own garland, 'and here we still are.'

*

The *Monterey* was steaming towards Pago Pago harbour in the American Samoan Islands, which lie to the north between Tonga and the Cook Islands. Trudie had loved this trip across the South Pacific Ocean, which had restored her faith in sea travel. This time she'd felt not a hint of sickness. The sea was behaving more like a river than an ocean. She was standing on deck with Jack, Bridget and Margaret. The four of them were silent, spellbound, as they watched their preconceived ideas of a tropical paradise emerge. There were sandy shores lined with coconut palms, rich green tropical vegetation and the most perfect harbour, almost landlocked and surrounded by great hills, one rising high into the sky with a rather flattened top.

'That must be "The Rainmaker",' said Jack, pointing. 'Pago Pago, of course, was Somerset Maugham's setting for his short story "Rain",' he added.

'Oh, Jack!' muttered Margaret. 'Don't be so pretentious.'

'Let's hope it *doesn't* rain,' said Bridget, laughing.

Trudie looked at Jack and thought she saw him redden a little. She felt protective towards him.

'Well, I'd like to read it sometime,' she said. 'I love reading books about places I've visited.'

'It's not really about the place itself,' continued Jack, smiling straight at her. 'It's about the clash between a puritanical missionary and a so-called *wanton* woman.'

'Wasn't there a film of it made with Margaret Lockwood?' Margaret asked, trying to be nicer.

They were interrupted now by the sight of the small boats coming out to collect them. The boats themselves were garlanded with flowers, as were the boatmen, and on board they could see yet more garlands of white flowers, hands of bananas and piles of coconuts.

'They must be for us,' Trudie said.

'Oh dear!' muttered Jack. 'Have we really got to wear them?'

Trudie was amazed at the water. She had never seen sea like this before, not in Ceylon or Australia, not at Kai Iwi beach at Wanganui, and not even on Fiji, where the skies were dark. This sea was a bright, light blue-green, not emerald, not even turquoise, more like opal, she thought. You could actually see brightly coloured tropical fish below the surface.

They arrived at the harbour and were greeted with a short welcome of local singing and dance and offered the choice of a guided tour round the island of Tutuila or free time to wander in the village here in Fagatoga, the largest settlement with the administration buildings. Jack immediately said he wanted to mooch about here, he didn't like guided tours. Trudie felt torn but decided to go with 'the girls' on the trip; she felt terribly self-conscious about her strong desire to be with Jack. Did the others suspect her feelings? As they drove past the US Naval Base and learned all about the coaling and repairs for the US Navy she regretted her decision. Although the bus was open-sided it was still stuffy in the heat and the twisty roads were making her feel sick. She remembered her walk with Jack round Toulon. She loved the way that he got so excited when he was exploring a new place. She wished she was with him now, out in the open taking a stroll by the sea.

She was relieved when the bus stopped at a lookout

above Atua village, where they could photograph views of the Rainmaker, or Atua as it was called locally. The guide explained how the mountain was seen as holy as its very height drew down the rain for the crops. From this view there was a huge panorama of the harbour. Trudie didn't even attempt a photograph. She knew her camera wasn't up to it. Instead she looked, she smelled, she listened. Was this the most beautiful view she'd ever seen? She wouldn't want dear old Dads to know this! Nothing but the view from Johnny Turner's of the banks of the Nith for him.

On the way back they stopped at a small stall to buy local fruits and beautifully crafted souvenirs and here she found a coloured photograph of the harbour for sale. 'Much better than I could do myself,' she said to Bridget, who was collecting some mementoes to take home.

*

On our first evening on Rarotonga I think this has to be as lovely as Pago Pago. Beyond the hotel are the golden palm-fringed sands, the coral reef and the stunning turquoise sea. Behind it is a narrow flat strip of market gardens and fruit trees which lead to the slopes of the one high mountain in the middle of the island. The Edgewater Resort is like a tourist hotel anywhere in the world, except for the setting. As we sit having a rum punch above the beach and the coral reef, we recite our little mantra: 'Better than the Holloway Road in the rain.'

Yet something is slightly unsettling and I can't put

my finger on it. I have that odd nervousness in my stomach that I used to get as a child when I was away from home. I called it 'homesickness' but it was more a physical anxiety than an emotional longing. I have it now. Is it disappointment that we never got to Pago Pago; that like so many things on this journey into the past it remains just out of reach? I try to describe these physical, emotional feelings, try to explain them to Lawrence.

'It's our trip coming to an end, and Jack and Trudie's, and most of all your exploration of their journey,' he says. 'It's no wonder you're feeling sad.'

'It's also just being tired. Tomorrow we'll have a brilliant day – just look at the reef for a start.'

'Yes, we can swim and snorkel and hire bikes and cycle all the way round the island and find a perfect spot for an evening meal.'

Dear Lawrence! He knows all the things to suggest that will cheer me up.

*

In the early evening the island people of Pago Pago prepared food for the foreigners from the ship and put on a cultural entertainment. The large ships stopped regularly and the islanders were skilled at knowing what visitors enjoyed. They set up canopies near the jetty so everyone got a view of the mountains and the sea. They cooked fresh fish, which was like nothing Trudie had ever tasted before. It was grilled on charcoal out in the open and flavoured with a spicy coconut sauce. There was an abundance of beautifully ripened bright yellow bananas of all shapes and sizes, some as small as your finger, and there were piles of fresh coconuts with straws stuck in so you could drink the juice without getting splashed. Trudie was sitting in her usual group with Margaret, Bridget and Jack. They exchanged their day's adventures. She got the impression that Jack had relished this day on his own to explore. She felt totally happy, now. After the heat of the day she loved the swift tropical evening and the coming of the warm, balmy night. The lights of the *Monterey* flickered on out at sea. She looked at the others. They were hypnotised too.

It was fully dark when the little boats took them back to the ship, but the light from the stars and the light from on board gave them a last view of the harbour. Back on the *Monterey* there was dancing. They all decided to meet in the ballroom after a quick change. They agreed it had been too good a day to let it finish early. Trudie felt just right to be there in Jack's arms for the waltzes and quicksteps. It was easy as she had partnered him so often on board the *Oronsay* and now on the *Monterey*. The difference in height didn't seem to matter any more. She felt she fitted well into his embrace.

Then they strolled out on to the deck and star-gazed. She was amazed by the stars in the southern hemisphere. Of course she knew them well by now, having spent weeks out on the sea. She knew where to spot Orion, the Great Bear, the Milky Way, the Southern Cross and the Evening Star, Venus. They were standing side by side, close but not touching, gazing up at the stars and out to sea. All her senses seemed on fire. She felt sick with nervous excitement, sure now that he must take her in his arms and kiss her. But he made no move. At last, she broke the silence – she had to.

'Jack, I'm so glad you're here.'

He looked down at her and gently stroked her cheek. Then he kissed her on the lips. It was a gentle kiss, not like the passionate kisses she remembered from Gabriel, but it turned her whole stomach upside down and she felt desire mixed with a yearning she'd never experienced before. He held her tightly in a strong embrace and whispered, 'I'm so glad you're here too.' He started to say more, then stopped. For what seemed to Trudie a long time they stood again looking out to sea, but close together now. She longed for him to kiss her once more.

He put his arm round her and led her gently back towards the ballroom. As they stepped through the doors from the deck he said, 'The others will be wondering where we are,' and laughed nervously. 'We don't want them jumping to the wrong conclusions,' he added.

*

The next day Rarotonga is grey and drizzly. I know it's the rainy season but it doesn't stop the disappointment. Everything that was once sparkling is dull: the sea is a dead green, all that colour has vanished. The hotel looks miserable and the few breakfast guests are huddled inside the café instead of outside on the terrace above the beach. They look so sorry for themselves.

'We could stay in our room and read,' Lawrence suggests, 'and check our emails.'

'I'd rather go out. We've only got today and tomorrow. We could do the hop-on bus trip round the island,' I suggest, 'and stop first in Avarua.'

Avarua is tiny, hardly the normal idea for a capital! But we find a good souvenir shop and buy some attractive bamboo bowls for our best friends that are painted the exact green that they love so they will fit into their decor; also they are light for us to carry. Then we continue our island trip despite the weather. Back on the bus I wonder what date it is today. I've lost track of time.

'It is 3 February today, isn't it?' I ask.

Lawrence checks his mobile, then remembers he hasn't changed it since New Zealand.

'We arrived on the first, Pacific time, because we left on the second, New Zealand time, so no, it's the second here today.'

'The third is my mother's birthday? I had thought for a moment it was today.'

'But it is the third today in England.'

'So it is ! She was born on 3 February 1911 and today in England is 3 February 2011. If she was alive she'd be a hundred years old!'

'And it must be over fifty years ago that she died, as you were nine.'

'Yes, nearly fifty-two years ago. She died in June, I think. Of course, if we're being precise it's only 4 am in the UK, twelve hours difference. I have no idea what time she was born.'

There are so many details I can never find out now, like the time of her birth. Yet I do feel that I'm beginning to get to know *her*, what she was like as a young woman.

*

That night in the harbour of Pago Pago, the night after dancing almost every dance with Jack and kissing him under the stars, Trudie couldn't sleep. She played it all back in her head. The day had been almost perfect, apart from the twisty road on the bus tour, but she felt hurt by Jack's final comment: 'We don't want them jumping to the wrong conclusions.' Why had it mattered what the others thought? And beneath it lay the implication that the moment, the kiss, would not have a conclusion, would never have the conclusion that she knew she wanted. She did know that he liked her. He had singled her out right from the beginning. She did know that he valued her friendship. They talked so well together. He listened to her ideas and seemed interested in what she had to say. Despite being less worldly, she did believe he respected her, her mind, her views, her values. It was she who partnered him most on the dance floor, who played him at table tennis and deck quoits. But he didn't love her! He really liked her, was fond of her, but he wasn't *in love* with her. Yet she still hoped. We're so much closer now than we were, she reasoned, I know he was really glad to meet me on the *Monterey* even though he'd never written. And we've got time yet, a couple of days in romantic Honolulu. He said he might join us on the trip to the Grand Canyon and New Mexico. And, after all, he kissed me! It must mean something.

Imagine Trudie's disappointment at they sailed on towards Hawaii and Jack distanced himself again. He would have explained to her that he intended to spend longer in Honolulu as he wanted to research and write a piece for the *Ethical Review* that he hoped to get published elsewhere, in a travel magazine. He had already booked his passage on the *Lurline* from Honolulu to San Francisco. She must have felt he was abandoning her, whatever he promised about meeting later in San Francisco, perhaps joining the group at the Grand Canyon or in Santa Fe, or maybe seeing her off on the *Queen Mary*.

She wrote home on 20 January, the day she left Honolulu without Jack. The letter ends:

Did I tell you there were nine of us on board of the original Oronsay party? Brother Holmes I'm glad to say is not amongst them though Brother Jack is or, I should say, was. He and two others are staying over at Honolulu for eight or nine days but I expect to see them in San Francisco and Jack will be in New York in time to see me off on the Queen Mary. *He is then having a month there with friends arriving home ten days before the start of the Easter holiday. Some people know how to manage things don't they? We are all going to meet at Whit for a week-end in the Lake District.*

I'm afraid my muse is not working this morning. Cheerio for the present and lots of love,
   GPL

No, her muse wasn't working. She must have been sad and disappointed and missing Jack, too, although I'm sure she put a very brave face on it and didn't let the others guess her feelings.

Jack wrote home nine days later:

Dear Mum and Dad,
In a day or two I shall arrive at San Francisco, and then it will be a long rush until New York. I have just spent 9 days in Honolulu and I fell in love with the place immediately. Oahu is like a garden island and Honolulu is a garden city, beautiful homes built amid coconut palms and hibiscus and other glorious shrubs. In the oriental quarter where the Japanese, Chinese, Koreans and Filipinos live everything is different and fascinating. Japanese girls, looking like sprigs of almond blossom, serve in the shops and restaurants where everything is displayed with exquisite taste. I was surprised at the beauty of the hula dance. To see the real thing helps you appreciate the artistry.

Did Jack have any intention of catching up with Trudie and her friends, whether in San Francisco or Santa Fe? He was clearly enjoying his travels on his own, admiring those pretty Japanese girls and dreaming perhaps about his lost loves. Maybe he had realised the depths of Trudie's feelings for him and was doing, in his view, the kindest thing.

*

That evening, after our rain-filled day travelling round Rarotonga by bus, there is local entertainment at our hotel and now it's beginning to really pour. I feel sorry for the drummers and dancers as they try to find shelter under the overhanging balconies where our room is.

'Aren't you coming to watch us?' they ask as we go

up the stairs to our room.

How to explain? How to say the last thing we want to do is to watch 'native' dancing and 'cultural' entertainment. Yet this is their livelihood. What Jack and Trudie experienced in Pago Pago would have been more authentic. Tourism, as we know it, had not really taken off then. Now an island like this survives on its tourism: holidays, weddings, honeymoons, the 'island experience' is now everyone's dream.

I tell them we are tired, we have seen so much of their beautiful island today.

'You're missing some fun,' a young girl giggles. 'You know, it's always even more fun when it rains!'

And rain it does. Lying in bed we can hear the storm coming in from the sea. Wind has always frightened me and tonight it is fierce. I fall asleep, then wake to hear the wind louder than ever beating the palms on the beach and rattling our shutters. Fear grips me as thoughts of a tsunami fill my head. Pictures on the news when the tsunami hit Pago Pago flash back to haunt me. I try and calm myself, and am determined not to wake Lawrence. This is stupid.

Then I see us under a bed in Haiti having been warned that Hurricane Frederick was coming. But Frederick veered off to the north. I comfort myself with that thought for a moment before the panic rises again. It's being on this tiny island in the middle of the Pacific, completely surrounded by hundreds of miles of sea. How can we escape?

Images of the huge Boxing Day tsunami come to mind. I see myself and Lawrence running desperately towards the mountain. I start to count sheep to try and calm myself, but my mind is racing. Why on earth did we come here to this place of rain and storms, this tiny speck in the middle of the Pacific?

I replay all the dreams I have had since childhood about what we then called tidal waves. I'm always running from the sea towards a mountain but my legs turn to jelly. A great wave hits me and pulls me under before I wake to find myself wrapped in a blanket or covered by my pillow. Were those recurring dreams some dreadful prophecy of my own end, of what is about to happen now? Why have we come here when we didn't need to? Have I gone and hit Jack's 'damn genie' right in the eye?

When I wake up, I can see sunlight through the shutters. Lawrence throws them open and we see all the colours again, perfect weather for our final day. Now we can bicycle round the island, snorkel in the lagoon, relax on the beach.

'Did you sleep well?' Lawrence asks.

We have found just the right place for our evening meal. We wanted it to be a bit special as this is our last night of the main part of our trip, the last night of the quest to discover Jack and Trudie. We will spend a short time on the west coast in the USA visiting family and friends, then fly home from San Francisco. Here is the hotel that we would have been staying in if we were rich. It's a short walk from the Edgewater. It's called the Crown Beach Resort.

It reminds us of our favourite hotel in Tobago, the Kariwak. Just like the Kariwak, it has separate thatched bungalows round a pool and a tropical garden. But unlike the Kariwak, it is right on the beach, with the coral reef beyond. We are watching the sun set as we sip our punches and reflect on the sudden changes of weather here, just like in Trinidad and Tobago. After all the rain yesterday and the stormy night with a raging sea, it is now perfectly calm. The evening sun is lighting everything up pink. Our charming waitress offers to take our photograph. It's too tempting to refuse, though we feel a little self-conscious.

'Now,' she says shyly, 'you have a lovely photograph to show your children.'

How to explain that sadly there are no children or grandchildren? How to explain the complex psychology of loss and regret? I smile and offer to take hers.

She tells us how she grew up on one of the smaller islands. She says she loves living here and has no desire to move to New Zealand like her cousins. She describes to us the beauty of her own home.

'If you think this is beautiful, wait until you see Puka Puka.'

As I hear the name I think about Pago Pago.

'Have you visited the Samoan Islands?' I ask. 'They are not far from here. Do you know of Pago Pago?'

She looks blank for a while and then she laughs. 'You mean Pango Pango,' she says.

'Is that how you say it, Pango Pango?'

'Yes,' she explains. 'It's the way we talk, it's our accents, it's how they say it themselves. The Samoans are very like us. The same people really. Have you been there?'

'No,' I reply, 'but my parents visited there a very long time ago, and my mother always called it Pango Pango.

"South Sea visitors."

She must have learned how to pronounce it correctly in the way that the local people spoke!'

When I asked my mother about the photograph on the mantelpiece, next to the one of my parents paddling when I was 'somewhere round the corner', she explained that it was special to her because it was where she first kissed my father. I'm not sure that as a young child I understood the difference between kissing like I did and the kisses of lovers. But I did understand that this place, Pango Pango, held a special memory for her. Of course she never told me the whole story and what must have happened after the kiss, how long she had to wait for the next one!

Pago Pago – 'the most beautiful harbour in the world'

CHAPTER 12 – Home

WE FLY BACK HOME FROM SAN FRANCISCO at the beginning of March 2011, seventy-two years after Jack and Trudie's return, and our life resumes. Occasionally I'm back again, thinking about the trip. First there's the terrible news of the Christchurch earthquake and the loss of Rod and Margot's home. They had a narrow escape, unlike many. Then Cosmo's grandson, Mark Manea, whom I contacted by email, thanks to the librarian's discoveries in Albany, sends me a picture of the Strand Café as it was in the 1930s when Trudie was there. Its Edwardian double-fronted bay windows are full of bowls of chocolates and it advertises jelly and ices. Mark tells me he lives at Donnybrook, just a stone's throw from Nannup. It's a pity I didn't know that before our trip. Yet Mark has little more to tell me about Cosmo or Spero; he too is trying to unravel his family history. However, this correspondence with him draws me back into the pleasures of discovery. I decide I must complete the story.

There's a huge gap in my parents' lives between 1939 and 1943. No letters have survived from that time. I hunt through every sheet of paper stuffed in the 'Pandora' trunk but I find nothing from then. I do come across the five letters that my grandmother wrote to her sister during the terrible summer of 1959, when my mother was dying. These are letters that I've hidden from myself since my father's cousin sent them to me years ago. I am now ready to read them. But for the early war years there are only small fragments that I am trying to make sense of.

I have a few snatches of memory and some references to Jack from the *Ethical Record*s. Then I discover, hunting among the old books in Lawrence's study, the *World Digest of Current Fact and Comment*, Vol. 2, No. 8, December 1939. On the cover is a pencil reference to page 45, where Jack's article, 'Half across the World by Boat and Bus – Honolulu to New York', is sitting rather uncomfortably between 'The Two G's Gestapo and GPU' and 'Goebbels: War-hater and Nature-Lover (condensed from an article written by the German Propaganda Minister in 1924)'.

Was this Jack's first publication beyond the *Ethical Record*? Is this what he stayed behind in Honolulu to research? Is this why travelling alone was preferable to travelling with my mother and her group of friends, Bridget, Muriel and Margaret?

After reading the opening section, I wonder if he was reminded of his evening in Pago Pago as he recalls the garlands from Honolulu:

They gave us each a lei to hang around our neck. The girls had garlands made of two or three kinds of flowers; mine was a neat firm masculine one made from a purple bloom. The band played Aloha Oe as the ship glided from the quay. In the evening we cast our leis into the sea. I watched mine swirl round and round before it disappeared, like a tiny vortex. Legend says that if the lei drifts ashore you will return.

My mother wrote her last letter home from the Grand Canyon: *Jack who is travelling by bus could not get here in time*. It's the last mention of his name. Did he see her off on the *Queen Mary* as he had promised?

I decide to visit Huddersfield. It may jog my memory, perhaps bring back some of the details my mother told me about her life after the *trip round the world*. My cousin Sue may have anecdotes to add or perhaps she has discovered more letters or old photographs from the past. Huddersfield, as well as being my mother's home, was also once a second home for me. I ring Sue to organise a visit.

'We can always start with the family grave,' Sue says. 'Remember how often we used to visit it when we were kids. Were we fascinated by death, do you think? Were we trying to understand it?'

I first met Death in Bosham, Hampshire. We were on holiday at Bracklesham Bay and I had been taken out by some friends to visit the tiny church where King Canut's daughter was supposed to be buried. I was only four and the crypt frightened me. The idea of dying and then being buried was totally new. When I got back to Mummy I had lots of questions but I didn't get any clear answers. Dying, being dead and being buried were all a puzzle and a muddle in my mind. A year later my grandfather 'Dads' died. My mother said that we had to go to Huddersfield immediately, just me and Peter, without Daddy, because 'Granddad is very poorly'. All the time she was talking she was crying, and Mummy never cried. Then I heard her telling Mrs Dyke, our next-door neighbour, about Grandad being deaf.

'Grandad's not deaf,' I said, 'but he is blind.'

'No, dear,' said Mrs Dyke. 'Mummy was talking about his death.'

Death remained a puzzle when we got to Huddersfield. 'Grandad's in heaven,' Cousin Sue explained. 'No, he's not,' argued Jane. 'He's still upstairs under a sheet and he'll be put in the ground for worms to come and eat him up.'

My mother tried to protect us, her two children, from the hurts of life and death. She had no idea then just how much we needed to be prepared rather than protected. Yet she had grown up with death not far away. I know from looking at the Pearce family tree, and from Bonny Landsborough's research, just how many young deaths there were in the family, due partly to the Great War.

Now I am standing in front of the Pearce family grave in the cemetery near Birkby, Huddersfield, looking at Grandad's name: 'Thomas Landsborough, beloved husband of Gertrude Pearce Landsborough, Died 5th January 1955'.

'This was the way we walked to school as kids. Do you remember? How long did you stay with us then, when Auntie Trudie was in hospital?'

'A couple of months maybe. I can't remember exactly. I've blocked out a lot of that time.'

'Every day we walked here through the cemetery and would stop off en route to say hi to our grandparents. Sometimes we'd pick flowers and stick them in a jam jar on the grave right here.' Sue points to a little stone shelf.

'It's odd, isn't it?' I muse. 'My mother was dying, which I think I was beginning to realise, yet I got pleasure from putting flowers on the grave of my grandparents.'

'Maybe, subconsciously, you were trying to come to terms with her death.'

We recite the names together. They somehow reassure us of our own existence. There is Great-grandfather Pearce, the jeweller, and Great-grandmother Pearce from the huge Short family, whose family tree I used in attempting to find the Antipodean Pearces. There's a little baby Pearce, Mary, who was my grandmother's sister. My grandmother Gertrude Pearce Landsbourough is buried here, 'Mumsie' as I now think of her. My mother, of course, was named after her. And there's Thomas, Trudie's beloved 'Dads'.

'Where was Auntie Trudie buried?' Sue asks.

'She wasn't. She was cremated. There was no memorial stone. Nothing. She just disappeared. Nobody really explained anything to me at the time. I don't know about Peter, what he was told or what he understood. Dad was so much in shock. My grandmother Annie was unwell herself and trying to support my father. I was sent away from home. It was awful.'

'It's so hard for children,' Sue says, thinking of her own kids. Her three weren't that different in age from me and Peter when George, her husband, died. I know she understands this need of mine to go back, to recreate the past.

After the cemetery we visit Birkby Primary, just down the road. From the outside the school is exactly as

I remember it: a low grey-stone building with the playground at the side and back. I spent half a term here trying to make sense of what I was learning in a class of forty where no one could understand a word I said and I couldn't understand the teacher. Yet I don't remember being particularly unhappy. I think school must have distracted me from the real worries of my life. And the kids were friendly and curious about the strange little girl with the posh southern accent who couldn't skip well, didn't know the skipping songs and had never played hopscotch.

'I think you three must have protected me,' I say to Sue. 'I don't remember anyone picking on me or being unkind.'

'No one would have dared tamper with a cousin of the three Landsborough girls.' They flash back into my mind, those strong, tall, attractive cousins of mine, as tough as any of the lads.

We stop in the back lane at 166 Trinity Street, where Uncle Henry and Auntie Peggy and their three daughters lived. Auntie Peggy finally moved out about fifteen years ago and went into a flat for the last few years of her life. We don't want to intrude on the Pakistani family who bought it, but they recognise Sue and insist on showing us round, pleased with their modernisations.

'What we couldn't understand,' the young man says, 'is what went on in the cellar. There were all these cages down there and tanks.'

'That's where my dad kept his alligators, his tropical fish and his snakes,' Sue explains. 'He'd be had up by the RSPCA if he was alive today.'

I loved staying in that house of women. It's no wonder Uncle Henry retreated to his hobbies in the cellar. Femininity dominated. The four of us girls could spend hours sitting in the bathroom putting on make-up and trying on clothes. Auntie Peggy's hairdressing salon was in the front room and provided yet more scope for beautification. It was so different from my home and I loved it.

Yet there are sad memories too. It was where I came during the first few weeks of my mother's illness. Being with her favourite brother and the sister-in-law she adored comforted me, as did the security I felt in the affection of my cousins. But, as I look into the bedroom now, the one where us four girls slept, I remember how I'd lie awake and listen to the late-night phone calls after the others had fallen asleep. Uncle Henry talking to my father, talking *about* my mother. Those hushed tones, the serious voice. It was here that I began to realise that my mother was going to die.

I'm sitting in the kitchen, watching television with Uncle Henry. We are watching Stirling Moss in *This is Your Life* and he's just been reunited with his sister. I hear a sniff behind me and I turn to see that Uncle Henry is crying. I know exactly why. My tears start and I run out of the kitchen and into the front room, where Auntie Peggy is hairdressing. Only she's not. She's talking to Auntie Bea. There's a horribly serious atmosphere. I rush into Auntie Peggy's arms and weep. I keep repeating, 'Please don't let my mummy die.' Auntie Bea creeps away. Auntie Peggy ends up promising that she won't let my mother die. And I believe her, at least for a while.

We drive on to Fitzwilliam Street. The houses at the bottom of the street are small. We stop at number 72, where the Landsborough family lived in 1911, the year my mother was born. Here, according to the census, there were ten people living in this small house: my grandparents and their four children, Susie, Alex, Henry and Trudie, my Great-aunt Mina, who was Thomas's much younger sister, two boarders, who were credit drapers working with my grandfather, and Annie Longley, the 'general servant, domestic'.

'It must have been tough for all of them,' Sue says, 'but imagine life for the servant, probably stuck in a garret or a basement. You know, I remember Auntie Mina quite well. I went with Dad to Crocketford once to stay in the croft. I loved it. Auntie Mina spoiled me to death.'

'Lucky you! I longed to go to Crocketford when I was a kid. My mother talked about it all the time. It was a romantic, beautiful place in my imagination. We should go together sometime. There's a churchyard there at Kirkpatrick where our family are buried. Bonny Landsborough sent me some interesting information. There are our great-grandparents and our great-aunts. Also there's a memorial to Auntie Mina's young husband, Private Norman Wilkinson, who died in the first war.'

As we walk up towards number 94 the houses get larger. Sue has already warned me that the house itself has gone. There's now a bridge over the new ring road, but she says that we can look at the other houses and see what we can remember as they are all very similar. We pause outside the house on the end, next to the bridge, the closest we can get to the original.

'Do you remember the golden wedding?' asks Sue. 'Number 94 was a rather nice hotel and they had the reception there. Grandma and Grandad had wanted to return to their old home. They lived with Auntie Susie and Auntie Bea in Quarmby when we were kids. Grandad had lost all the money.'

'I wonder what they made of Auntie Susie and Auntie Bea? After all, they did share a room, didn't they? The big one with the huge beams and the double bed?'

'Yes. There were only two bedrooms. Of course nobody ever *said* anything. Poor Bea. I think she got a hard deal, family but not family. Nowadays it'd be so different.'

'Can you remember our grandfather, Sue?'

'I know he was a great one for teasing.'

I look closely at the house in front of me and it's the steps that come back, those steep wide steps.

'I remember going up steps just like these. And a big hall or reception room and lots of grown-ups I didn't know and my mother talking and talking to everyone. I can just see Grandad. He walked very slowly with a stick. He was nearly blind, of course, and physically quite crippled. My mother told me how damaged he'd been by the Great War.'

'Maybe that's why he couldn't make it in business. I know my father had longed to study medicine but there was just no money.'

'My mother told stories about Grandad, their adventures together. She really loved her family. I've learned that from the letters you found, as well as from what I can remember. It's clear how much she missed them in Australia even though she was having a great adventure.'

'Such a long time to be so far away from family,' Sue says. 'I can imagine her delight in getting home. I always feel good when I get back to Huddersfield.'

*

Trudie arrived in England on 5 March 1939. Mumsie and Susie were at Tilbury to meet her and they spent the weekend at Auntie Emily's in Chiswick. Trudie was due straight back to her teaching post in Birmingham. Euston Station was packed and she was shocked to see so many young men in uniform. The possibility of war was everyone's subject of conversation now. As she waved goodbye to Mumsie and Susie, Trudie had to blink back her tears. She so wanted to be with her family at this moment when she was feeling so strange, with all her emotions awry: thrilled to be home but missing the life that she had been living, the friends that she had made.

By the time the Easter holidays arrived she was back into the swing of things. She'd had the challenge of taking over her classes from the Australian exchange teacher, Miss Richards. She was exhausted but relieved that she had coped. In fact, she had managed in these few weeks to get to know her classes, learn all their names, understand their different needs and get them adjusted to her methods of teaching in geography, maths and PE. She left for Huddersfield the afternoon that term finished. It was sixteen months since she'd stepped foot in 94 Fitzwilliam Street, and as long since she'd seen her beloved Dads! Of course they had spoken on the telephone, but that wasn't always easy, arranging the time for him to be at Alex's to take the call.

Dads was there on Huddersfield Station to meet her, along with Alex, who had just started his own taxi business and would drive them home.

'My own wee darling daughter,' Dads said as he hugged her and broke down crying.

'Oh, Dads.' Trudie held on to him tight. He suddenly seemed so old and frail, even though he was only fifty-five.

Back at Fitzwilliam Street, after Trudie had played with Sally, inspected the garden and looked at the little changes made in the house, she sat down to tea with her family, just like old times. There was so much news to catch up on. Cousin May was about to be married and Trudie and Susie were to be bridesmaids. Henry had joined the navy and was dating a pretty local girl called Peggy. They weren't sure it would last once he was at sea. Alex and Kathleen were planning on buying a house in Birkby.

'The big news is,' said Susie mysteriously, 'we might be thinking about moving!'

'Oh no! Why?'

'Well, darling', said Mumsie, 'you've all gone now apart from Susie. It's too big for us and really we could do with the cash.'

'I'm afraid my business is finally finished,' Dads said. 'After I declared bankruptcy in '35 I just couldn't get going again. Hadn't the heart.'

'Poor Dads,' Trudie said.

She knew only too well how he'd struggled with his bad health, added to which he just didn't have a particularly good head for business – he was far too soft. Then she thought of her mother. How she must feel it! All those successful Pearce brothers: Henry the jeweller of Pearce and Sons, Charlton in a good business in Wanganui, John thriving in Perth and Ernest doing well as an accountant. Her own husband was a failure.

'When will this happen?' she asked them softly.

'Oh, not for a while,' Susie explained. 'We want to find somewhere that costs little but we can make really nice. Bea has offered to help me look. She knows a lot about properties.'

It felt strange to Trudie that Susie now seemed to be the head of the family. She found herself resenting it a little. Her parents weren't that old yet. She excused herself quickly after tea and went up to her old room, which was now used as the study, sewing space and store for some of her father's unused cloth. She was sad. She had imagined coming home to everything exactly as it had been, but everyone and everything was different: Dads old and down, Mumsie even more quiet than usual and Susie bossier than ever. This new friend of Susie's, Beatrice Hall, or Bea as Susie called her, why was she so involved in everything as if she was one of the family?

She sat down on her bed and noticed a letter propped on the bedside table addressed to her. She knew the handwriting at once. It was Bridget's.

My Dear Trudie

I hope your half term was alright. Mine was awful but more of that anon. I wanted to let you know quickly that the Bradford girls, Muriel and Margaret, and I have planned to meet in the Lakes for a walking holiday in the Whitsun break. We very much hope you can come. We plan to ask Jack, too. I'm sure you'll be pleased about that! But not Holmes. Let us know as soon as possible if you can make it.

Love and Best Wishes,
Bridget

The heavy, sickening feeling of depression lifted, to be replaced by excitement. It would be wonderful to meet up again with everyone and share memories, share photographs, share that life once more. It would be lovely to see the girls, though 'girls' was not really how she thought of Muriel and Margaret. And as for Jack? She doubted he'd come this far north at Whit. And did she want him to anyway? Did she want to stir up her heart again?

She was woken from her thoughts by a brisk knock. Susie came in and sat down next to her on the bed, putting an arm around her.

'Trudie, dear, I'm so happy to have you home. I've missed you more than you can imagine.'

'And me you, dearest Toozle.' How could she have had those mean thoughts?

'I want to hear everything, every single thing about your trip. And what happened to that young man? The writer chap?'

Trudie giggled. 'He was never a writer, Susie, just a

teacher like us who wants to be a writer. And anyway, I doubt I'll ever see him again.'

'Why ever not?'

'It's a long story. I shall tell you all about it in time.'

*

About the same time in London, at 78 Underhill Road, Forest Hill, Dulwich, Jack was reading a similar letter inviting him on the walking holiday in the Lake District over the Whitsun break. He couldn't decide if he would go or not. On the one hand it would be fun to relive some of the experiences of the journey. He would like to see his fellow exchange teachers again, especially Trudie Landsborough. But she was the problem too. He didn't want to lead her up the garden path. He knew she was fond of him, and more. But he just wasn't in love with her in that passionate, obsessive way he had been with Joyce for ten long years and, if he was totally honest, still was. Nor did she compare with the beautiful New Zealand girl he had left behind in New Plymouth. And yet... there was something. She was sympathetic, intelligent, thoughtful. And she did have lovely eyes. He decided to talk it through with his mother. She was a wise woman who had been a great confidante over his love for Joyce.

His mother was at the piano, preparing for her week's piano lessons. She smiled at him. 'Let's go and sit in the garden, Jack, and enjoy this spring weather now it has arrived.'

They sat out on the old wooden bench under the oak tree. Jack surveyed the garden, which was exactly as he remembered it: the daffodils and tulips were out in the borders, the white lilac was in bloom, the grass looked perfectly mown and rolled. The potting shed was crammed with Dad's seedlings: so English, so London, so home.

'It's lovely being home,' he said. 'Dad is still enjoying the garden, I see.' He turned to his mother.

'He's beginning to find it a lot on top of all the Conway Hall stuff. That's what I wanted to discuss with you, dear. We've been thinking about dividing the house, making it into two flats. It would bring in some extra income and we could share the garden. To be honest with you, I'm also tired of traipsing all over London to teach piano. Nothing immediate, but in a year or two perhaps. See how things work out, see what happens with this possibility of war. We may all have to leave London, who knows?'

'What about me and Sydney?' Jack asked, a little peeved.

'Time you both moved out, settled down, started families. You're both so fussy. Didn't you meet any nice girls on your trip?'

'I met a lovely girl in New Plymouth,' he said, 'She was beautiful, intelligent and such a talented teacher. I wanted to bring her back with me. I would have loved to have married her. First she said yes, but then she changed her mind at the last minute. It was pressure from home partly. I don't blame her or her parents. How could she leave New Zealand to come here now?'

'My poor Jackie,' his mother said as she felt for his hand, 'You're such a romantic. You always want what you can't have. There's Eileen at Conway Hall, she's been keen on you for years. Though now I hear she's dating solid old Colin Barralett.'

'I did meet someone on the *Oronsay* going out and accidentally met her again on the way back. I know she likes me but I'm just not sure. I might go and meet her in the Lakes with the rest of the group. But I don't want to hurt her. What do you think?'

'Dear Jack, you have to decide that for yourself.'

I know that Jack's mother was hoping he'd settle. I have it in writing from my father's cousin Philippa, who wrote a piece for me about her memories of my mother:

Auntie Helen Lawrance first mentioned your mother, Trudie, to us. She said that Jack Green had met a girl on the boat to Australia and accidentally encountered her again on his voyage back. He seemed a little interested in her but his mother, Helen's cousin Annie, of whom she was extremely fond, didn't think there was anything in it as 'Jack was always difficult to please.'

Everybody loved Grannie Annie, Annie Green, born Annie Lawrance, the middle child and eldest daughter in a family of eight with no mother. She learned mothering from early, looking after her little sister Winnie and her six brothers. My father's father was apparently rather distant and quite strict – 'You could never just enjoy yourself,' Dad reminisced. 'You had to do a good long walk before lunch to earn it, and another after to pay for it!' But Annie was a mother who gave all. And not just a mother, but an aunt, a great-aunt and a grandmother whom everyone seemed to love. It annoyed me as a little girl that she was my cousin Mike's Grannie too. He adored her as I did and I resented the sharing. I remember saying, 'How can she be your grandmother when she's mine?'

It was she who came to the rescue during my mother's illness and death. Annie upped and left her home at 78 Underhill Road, Dulwich, where she still lived in the bottom half of the house, and came to Shrewsbury. Of course, I didn't realise then the sacrifice she was making. It separated her from her life in London and her dear sister Winnie.

5/6/59

Dear Win,

I can't say how sorry I was not to have written but I know you realise the position I am in. My heart seems to ache all the time. Trudie still lingers not in pain but lost to the world. Jack manages to visit and keep his end up fairly well but yesterday he looked awful. He just said, 'Horrible, how can I go again?' Peter is deeply depressed and in bed with a bad attack of asthma. Jennifer is on the farm with her little friend, Jill Brisbourne. I think they will be better soon, once Trudie is gone, it's the mystery of their mother still living and never coming home.

I have so much anxiety over dear Jack. When he is less strained, as when he is cooking, he is such a dear and so sweet to live with. He has fixed up for the children to be at friends and Trudie's family all summer so I can come home for a month. There is so much more to say Win, my dear, but it must wait. I just long to be home.

Much love, old Win,
Annie

It was her last visit. She returned to us in the September and was dead by Christmas. She never returned to her old home in Dulwich.

*

By September 1939 the war had started and life was turned upside down. Jack had to move from Dulwich and leave his dear mother, Annie, whether he liked it or not. I discovered this in the article from the December 1939 issue of the *Ethical Review*: 'Some Thoughts on Evacuation'. My father describes the relatively successful evacuation he was part of when chaperoning his school pupils from London to Godden Green in Kent.

I have experienced none of the dreadful things that we have read about in newspapers: London Children out of control, or country people serving up grilled squirrel for breakfast. Let me say frankly that we have had no cause for a grouch. We have been lucky. If every community of evacuees had been received with the care and kindness accorded to us, the scheme would be an unqualified success.

He was part of that great exodus of teachers and pupils from London schools on 1 September 1939.

For my mother I have no archive material at all from the early war years. I do remember her telling me stories about being in Birmingham and seeing bombs dropping. She told me about that night in 1940 when the bombs fell on Coventry. She had a longing to see the new cathedral and went to see the laying of the first stone in 1956, but she never lived to see the cathedral completed, never experienced the beauty and sadness of seeing the bombed skeleton of the old cathedral set against the new church.

I remember that phrase so well, 'during the war we...', but what came next I have no idea despite the constant references to that time during my early childhood. To unlock those memories now seems impossible. Vague pictures come into my head, such as going to Birmingham with my mother and visiting two old ladies who lived in an upstairs flat. I can see the blue door we went through on the side of a house. But no more. The little green address book gives me no clues. There are addresses of friends in Birmingham, many in Moseley and perhaps her school was there. I contacted the League of Commonwealth Exchanges, but received remarkably little information. There is a list of the exchange teachers for 1938 which includes Miss G. P. Landsborough and Mr J. L. Green, alongside those familiar names I now know: Miss B. Battersby, Miss M. R. Sandilands, Miss M. Petyt, Miss M. E. Cocking, Mr F. A. Holmes. But there are no references to their schools.

What I did learn, though, from the Commonwealth League was that the next group of teachers, those who started teaching in the spring of 1939, never got back during the war and some settled out there for good. What luck, what chance it is that Jack and Trudie were not there one year later, Trudie stranded in Western Australia and Jack stuck in New Zealand.

*

Sue sends a copy of a photograph she has found of her parents' wedding in March 1942. I remember it in the old box of family photos that my mother kept in the sideboard, or a photo that was very similar. In this one there's no top-hatted Uncle Henry, it's of the bride and her bridesmaids. Peggy is in a swirl of white, looking quite lovely. In front is a little bridesmaid also in white. The two other bridesmaids, Peggy's sister Joyce and my mother, look rather drab – 'war utility' in more sombre colours, brown on the brown and white photograph. Joyce is beaming but Trudie looks sad, a small, thin little figure without a smile. Maybe she's thinking, 'A bridesmaid for Kathleen, a bridesmaid for Cousin May and now a bridesmaid for Peggy. Three times a bridesmaid is never a bride.'

'Still not a bride'

CHAPTER 13 – Hartrigg House

JACK WAS SITTING IN HIS LOCAL PUB, the Red Lion in Barnes, just a stone's throw from his digs in Crestway, on a Friday evening in March 1943. He liked to have a pint of ale after his busy day. It was school until late afternoon, then teaching three evenings a week at Royal Holloway. He knew he was lucky to be teaching adult evening classes in psychology. The extra money was useful, but more importantly it was a step towards changing his career, becoming an educational psychologist. Yet he had no time for living, no way of meeting new people. He really felt rather depressed with life. If only this damn war would be over. He was sorry he'd not been fit enough for service. At least he would be doing something useful. Yes, teaching was necessary, but sometimes it all seemed a waste of time. And Sloane School, now West London Emergency School, was dreary. Old-fashioned. The acting headmaster, old Kingsford, was a war stand-in not interested in any new ideas. German was unpopular now as an A-level subject, though God knows they might all need it. Most of his teaching was English, but English of the most traditional kind, too much parsing and not enough literature!

He picked up his book, *Of Human Bondage*, and reread the ending again: 'But Philip wrenched the pang (Mildred) from his heart. He thought of Sally, with her kind blue eyes; and his lips unconsciously formed themselves into a smile.'

The novel was speaking to him. Like Philip, he had been obsessed with one woman and taken the other for granted. Was Joyce his Mildred? Not a woman of 'questionable virtue', as in Maugham's novel, but a woman who could never love him. Every time he saw her he would feel that pang, even though now they were just good friends and he had grown quite fond of her partner, Jane. It was time to 'wrench that pang'. It was time to live in the present. Like Philip in the novel, he should stop dreaming, stop living in some unreachable future while he let the present slip away. He knew who his Sally was, his girl with the blue eyes. She had been popping up in his thoughts a lot, filling his mind with regrets. Why had he followed her across America without catching her up? Why hadn't he joined the exchange teachers' group in the Lake District that Whitsun before war was declared? Why, when Trudie had still written, in her friendly, down-to-earth manner, had his responses been short, undeveloped and merely polite? In her last letter, a year ago, she had sent him her new address at a boarding school in Yorkshire. She had left Birmingham during the worst period of the Blitz. Could he, should he, make a move?

It was interesting psychologically, he thought, that now, when he'd probably left it too late, he really wanted her. He remembered how well they'd got on. How they could talk together for hours. Why hadn't he realised it four years ago? Because he was besotted by beauty and by the unobtainable. Joyce, of course. And his lovely New Zealand girl, who had given him up for the life that she knew, for the chap she was sure of. Quite right too!

He should never have expected her to follow him to Europe in 1939. It was he, Jack, who was the chump.

He finished his beer and walked home full of indecision. Should he write to Trudie? There was no point now in beating about the bush. Heaven knows where they'd all be in a year or two. He shuddered as he thought of Hitler's remorseless advances. Life now seemed urgent rather than leisurely. Had he behaved just too badly? He must talk it over with someone. He decided he'd go to Dulwich early tomorrow morning and see his mother. He would be totally honest with her. Now he'd admit what a fool he had been about Trudie. His father was at Minehead on a walking holiday, so this was a good chance. He couldn't bear for his father to judge him.

*

Trudie had escaped to her freezing little room to avoid the dreaded Mrs Miller. Poor Mrs Miller had indeed had an awful life and Trudie had been very kind to her, taking her home last holiday, but she had to admit she was an awful bore. 'I always do it,' she said to herself. 'I'm always taking on lame ducks.'

She could hardly believe how miserable life had become. All the fault of this bloody war. Four years ago she was leaving the States on the wonderful *Queen Mary* after the most exciting time of her life. Now she was stuck in a girls' boarding school, Oaklands, run for war evacuees, on the moors outside Ilkley. She was teacher and general help. She had to be prepared to put her hand to everything. And she felt she couldn't even complain! She had a job, was fed and watered. She was one of the lucky ones. She had been sorry to leave Birmingham and her life there, but as the bombing intensified and the doodlebugs plagued them, and she got quite run down from lack of sleep, she realised, for the sake of her family if not herself, she should move back to Yorkshire. She missed her friends and her independent life. This was like being back at school and she was now thirty-two years old.

Someone knocked at her door. She nearly didn't answer, afraid it was Mrs Miller. As the knock came a second time and a girl's voice said 'Miss Landsborough?' she opened it. Young Mary Broadhouse was standing there holding a letter. 'Sorry to disturb you, miss, but miss said this came for you this morning and it got put aside by mistake.'

'Thanks, Mary, dear,' Trudie said as she took the letter and immediately recognised the familiar scrawl of Jack's handwriting. She tore the letter open the minute she shut the door.

Dear Trudie,
Have you ever read 'Of Human Bondage' by Somerset Maugham? I ask this because it does to some degree tell my own story, and you would realise that not only the stress of changing times, but also the necessity of getting something out of my own system, has prevented me from writing to you till now. Those days weren't wholly carefree.

She felt ready to laugh and cry. Silly Jack! Dear Jack! Always the intellectualiser! Somerset Maugham indeed.

She read on rapidly and discovered that he was determined they should meet over the Easter holidays. He spoke of wanting to come to Yorkshire, but not, necessarily, to her family. His whole letter implied seriousness. This seemed more than renewing a friendship. The letter had an urgent tone: *I'm determined to see you at all costs.* What has made him decide this now? She was perplexed. She longed to talk it through with someone. But who? No way could she discuss it with Susie. Susie had decided to disapprove of Jack right from the very beginning, referring to him as 'that journalist man'. Susie knew how disappointed Trudie had been in Jack's disappearance from her life after the year's exchange. She wished now she'd not confessed so much. Susie, who had little time for men anyway, would strongly advise her not to get involved again.

Surely there was no harm in meeting him? They could spend a little time together somewhere on their own. They were big people after all. She blushed as she thought of her own lack of experience with men. 'Who knows now what's coming in these uncertain times? I know I can love this man,' she thought, 'and what a delight to get far away from Miss Perry, Miss Bahlman, Matron and Miss Miller.'

She sat down and replied straight away, agreeing to meet him for a short holiday in Yorkshire. She suggested the Dales. It was one of her favourite places for walking and far enough away from Huddersfield for her to feel totally free from Susie's disapproval. She promised to find a good and reasonable place for them to stay. That night she didn't sleep at all, thinking about Jack's sudden reappearance in her life and what it might mean. She hadn't yet posted the letter. Should she tear it up? Should she not reply to him at all? Pay him back for his long silence? Yet she knew he was a good man. And she knew she loved him. She finally made a resolution before sleep came: 'I'll definitely book two single rooms. I wouldn't want Jack to think I'm desperate!'

Trudie was amazed at the speed of Jack's reply. His response came by return of post. She hadn't had a moment to herself. It had been a dreadful day. It wasn't till after supper that she snatched a moment to read it:

My Dear Trudie,
Wonderful to get your letter. Of course I'm not worried about your stray white hairs! You haven't changed. Anyway 'plus ca change, plus c'est la meme chose.' And what about my grey hairs, and scanty equipment thereof?

I was thrilled by your suggestion of the Dales. I have never yet been to Yorkshire. And I should love you to come to London soon. It's lovely to think that we shall meet.

She noted the 'my' at the beginning of the letter and the invitation to London. London! Well, the worst of the bombing had stopped now. Hopefully the Blitz really was over. The rest of the letter gave her a glimpse of his life there. It seemed so much more exciting than hers. Psychology seminars at London University, trips to the cinema, visits to the pub, interesting people. What on earth had she to offer? Well, she'd just have to tell him what life here was like.

Dear Jack,

I'm writing this in bed – what a day I've had. They rang up from the food office this morning for all the ration books and identity cards. Evidently they had asked Matron on Monday to send them at once but she had put it off then had to rush off to her sister who has received bad news of her son. I spent the whole morning on the job, getting the children to sign their books, checking addresses and hunting for lost identity cards. Poor Matron is a muddler and Miss Perry will have nothing to do with ration books. Really, Jack, your life sounds wonderful! Don't think I'm moaning but life as a teacher, cook, and child-minder wrapped into one is no joke. This evening I was switching from exam marking to cutting loaves of bread!

I am most certainly looking forward to our Easter holiday and will set about now exploring possibilities.

Goodnight, pleasant dreams,

Trudie

She decided that she would have to tell her family. They were expecting her home for Easter. Dads would be terribly disappointed. Mother and Susie would certainly disapprove. She decided she'd broach the subject with Susie by getting her recommendations on where to stay. Susie had been walking in Wharfedale quite recently with her good friend Beatrice Hall. She tried to imagine Jack meeting her family, but he was in a totally different compartment. What on earth would he make of them? Or they of him? 'I'll cross that bridge if I have to,' she said out loud to herself.

*

'And what about my grey hairs and scanty equipment thereof?'
Jack, 1943

A year has passed since we arrived home and it's now February 2012. I have started writing everything up, but I've not yet looked at the 'courtship letters'. Now I hunt through all the research material to find them. I'm suddenly very curious because I've just finished *Of Human Bondage*. It was in the collection of grey-green-covered Maugham books in Lawrence's study, as I had remembered on that visit to Raffles over a year ago. As I open the third letter from Trudie I notice something still in the envelope, wedged in. It's a very small letter or notelet which I hadn't noticed before. It's faded yellow with black ink and a clearly printed address in black lettering:

Hartrigg
Buckden,
Skipton in Craven

It's dated 29 March and is handwritten:

> **H**ARTRIGG,
> **B**UCKDEN,
> **S**KIPTON-IN-**C**RAVEN.
> *March 29*
>
> *Dear Madam,*
> *I shall be pleased to accommodate you from the 17th to 22nd. I'm afraid I can't keep you to the 24th. My terms are 10/ per day. An early reply will oblige.*
> *Yours Faithfully,*
> *C. M. Wight*

Dear Madam,
I shall be pleased to accommodate you from the 17th to 22nd. I'm afraid I can't keep you to the 24th. My terms are 10 shillings per day. An early reply will oblige.
  Yours Faithfully,
  C. M. Wight

So this is actually where they stayed! I decide to give it a google just on the off chance and there it is on Tripadvisor: 'Hartrigg House Best B&B', with a photo of an old stone house. I begin to imagine us going there and staying in the exact same room as my parents, though how I would know which one that is I have no idea, seventy years on. I notice the date that they planned to go, from 17 to 22 April. We shall go then!

I rush downstairs to tell Lawrence of my discovery. I'm ridiculously excited. It all fits together as he has to be at a conference in Leeds around that time.

The phone number doesn't work. After more research on Tripadvisor I ring a B&B nearby and they tell me they think Hartrigg has just closed down. If only I'd checked the letters a few months back! I should know by now how quickly disappointment can follow discovery. I can see that empty plot at Cottesloe, only the fig tree left, the ugly building in Albany where the Mount once stood. And even when you do find somewhere, like Jack's digs in Dunedin, what does it give you?

But I continue to search. On 'Addresses UK' I get a phone number to ring.

'No, madam, we gave up doing B&B at Christmas. We ran this place for many years and now we are retired.'

I tell him my story and he promises we can look around the house if we visit the area. 'At least that's something,' I say to Lawrence. 'I'll book the other B&B which looks really nice.'

It's Sunday 15 April when we drive from York to Wharfedale. It's a clear day with a bright blue sky but very cold for the time of year. We turn into the valley and pass Fountain's Abbey.

We're surprised how far it is to Buckden. A sunny Sunday has brought out visitors and the long winding road up the valley is busy.

'It wouldn't have been like this then,' I say. 'Imagine it in 1943 in the middle of the war with petrol shortages and lack of funds.'

'How do you think they got here?' Lawrence wonders.

'Must have been by train, then bus. I imagine they met in Skipton. Jack could have got a train there from London and Trudie from Huddersfield. Then they'd have got a bus, like that one we've just passed which is going right up the valley.'

'It would have been rather an awkward meeting if they'd not seen each other for four years. I bet they both felt incredibly shy.'

'I wish I had some more references to the actual holiday, details of what they felt when they first met.' I reach for my little pack of letters. 'Trudie wrote to Jack on 1 April confirming the holiday:

I have fixed up rooms for our holiday. I was very tempted to choose 'The Buck' but Susie assures me the rooms there are very cold. A friend of hers has stayed at Hartrigg and strongly recommends it, the food she says is particularly good so that's the one I've chosen. I hope it will be OK. I wonder what the weather will be like.

'He replies by return of post expressing his excitement:

The weather should stay fine. It is hot now in London. I've just walked all up Holland Park Road to Nottinghill and across the gardens to South Kensington where I called in at the 'Denmark'. They had placed daffodils all around the saloon. I felt a stirring of longing, old nostalgias, and then I thought this spring is Yorkshire and you and the present seems so good and full of promise.'

We park in the car park of the Buck. I'm convinced Jack and Trudie must have at least had a few drinks here, knowing my dad. But the pub is closed so we can't join them here. Over the road at Hartrigg House there's no sign of life. I should have given them another ring but I'd suddenly felt shy. This 'going back in time' slightly embarrasses me. What seemed part of our whole project on our world trip seems a little indulgent here in England. We walk up the drive and ring the bell, but no one answers. We peer through the windows. There's dark wood furniture and heavy curtains. It's old-fashioned and chintzy. It must be rather like it was back then.

The grounds are attractive with good views across to the hills. I take photographs of the house and garden and the old B&B sign, which is still hanging at the front. I feel a little disappointed and cross with myself that I didn't phone again to arrange the visit. What does it matter if people say no, and the owner had offered a visit on the phone anyway. Yet I have to admit to Lawrence that I'm rather glad we didn't actually stay here. It's a little bleak, as these large, dark, stone Yorkshire houses can be, perhaps a little too unchanged.

'I wonder if they used one room or two?' I muse, looking up at the bedroom windows. 'They probably started in two and ended up in one!'

They spent a week here walking the Dales. We have a day. We set out from the Buck and walk up on to the ridge that will take us to Cray and on to Hubberholme. The spring flowers are out, primroses and violets, and everything is lit by the bright sun. We can see right across the valley to Hubberholme and can make out one or two walkers on the track. There's a freezing wind and I'm regretting the lack of my fleece. We left London in warmth. At the top there are patches of snow on the ground and a few flutters in the wind. I remember in one of Jack's letters he talks about collecting his wind-jacket, rucksack and walking boots from home in Dulwich. Unfortunately we haven't got the right gear at all. By the time we get to Cray we are shivering. We notice how few walkers there are on the route but the pub is packed. Everyone seems to have driven. We thaw out in the pub with piping-hot potato and leek soup and then decide to return to our car. We can't bear the thought of getting cold again. We drive back down the valley to Kettlewell rather than continuing the walk to Hubberholme.

We drive on into Littendale towards our B&B and discover the little village of Arncliffe. There's an old-fashioned pub, the Falcon, that seems the ideal place for supper. Lawrence pops in to book a table and returns looking pleased.

'It's quite small and they usually do dinner just for their own guests, but as we're staying at Warren House they say it's OK. It's all local stuff cooked on an Aga.'

'Perfect.'

Our room at Warren House has a wide view of fields and hills and it's absolutely quiet. The room and bathroom are 'boutique' and there's a welcome flask of sherry to warm us. Disappointment about Hartrigg has certainly gone! Stepping back in time is all very well in theory. We've been following Jack and Trudie around the globe, so we are experienced in disappointments and miscalculations.

'Remember our night at the Galle Face?'

'That room like a storage freezer, the aircon gone mad!'

We reminisce about our own voyage as we watch the sun set over the hills, warm and cosy in our luxury room.

When we arrive at the Falcon I see Jack and Trudie here. The dining room hasn't changed in years. It is small and wonderfully old-fashioned: a bookcase filled with old books, a carriage clock on the mantelshelf, high-backed oak chairs and heavy faded velvet curtains. The new owners say they are going to modernise gradually.

*

Trudie and Jack spent their days in the Dales walking and talking. The weather was warm and full of spring promise. They had four years to catch up on. Four years of the war. Both had experienced the bombing and life in air raid shelters. Jack described his evacuation, that dramatic day in September 1939 when he'd been ordered, along with thousands of London teachers, to accompany their pupils to the country.

'It was surprisingly calm,' Jack recalled, 'despite what the papers said, 'but I don't think many of the children fully realised what it meant. I was lucky to end up near Sevenoaks, easy to return to London. It was a little village called Godden Green. The villagers had the shock of their lives when those city kids arrive en masse!'

'What happened?'

'It was awful, when we all arrived at Sevenoaks. We were impounded in the cattle market, where children were put five in a pen. But when we were divided up into smaller groups and deposited at our village, things improved. Teachers and children were given tea and biscuits at the school. Then we were all transported to our separate billets by the local gentry.'

'It sounds better than some stories I read in the papers. How long did everyone stay?'

'The kids drifted back to their families after the worst of the Blitz. I stayed on until I was officially able to return, almost a year. Then, after a bit of filling in, I got the job at Sloane School, West London Emergency, as it is officially called now.'

'I wasn't evacuated from Birmingham as some teachers and pupils were. My school was in Moseley, not right in the centre. I was building a life there and I got used to the patterns of interrupted nights. But it was the cumulative effect of the bombs and the doodlebugs and no sleep which eventually made me ill. My parents insisted that I move back to Yorkshire and be nearer them. I still don't like the job. The school, Oaklands, is not much more modern than Lowood Hall in *Jane Eyre*! It's halfway up Ilkley Moor, a good walk to the town. Until you got back in touch, Jack, I was feeling unutterably miserable.'

Jack stopped in his tracks and hugged her. What he valued most about Trudie was her honesty. She was direct. He hoped he could live up to her expectations of him.

On their last day they were sitting in the Falcon at Arncliffe, having sandwiches and a drink after a the long walk from Buckden, via Cray and Hubberholme.

'We might as well get married as soon as possible. Why wait?' Jack said.

'How soon?' asked Trudie, filled with that mixture of excitement and fear at the speed of change.

'August holidays?'

'But you haven't even met my family,' Trudie said, with her practical common sense, 'and I haven't met yours.'

'You must come to London at Whit and stay with my parents in Dulwich. My mother is dying to meet you. You'll love Annie Green!'

'I'd really like that,' Trudie said, 'but you will have to meet my family first.' She insisted. 'Why don't you come back with me? We have a few more days' holiday before school.'

Jack hesitated. He dreaded meeting Trudie's family. There were lots of reasons, but it was mainly that he felt they must know of his dalliance and indecision. Sister Susie was clearly a powerful woman and very protective towards her little sister.

'As long as you're not feeding me to the lions,' he said.

Trudie laughed. 'Mumsie and Dads are hardly that,' she said, 'but you'd better watch out for my sister!'

As they walked back to Hartrigg they both knew that now was the time. This evening, their last, it would be one room, one bed, one heart.

*

Over our last glass of wine at the Falcon I tell Lawrence what I can remember of Jack's story of his first visit to Huddersfield.

'He told me how he nearly didn't go through with the marriage after he met the Landsboroughs. Well, it was really Susie, I think. He thought my grandfather 'harmless enough'. Of course, Grandad was a bit of a tippler, liked his whisky, which would have recommended him to Dad, though Dad thought him 'eccentric'. He thought my grandmother disapproved of him as a future husband for her daughter. She was a teetotaller, wore the white ribbon. Dad always got on with Henry and Peggy, he really liked them. Well, you remember them, don't you?'

'They were charming. Your Uncle Henry rather dapper, if a little eccentric too. I remember how elegant he always looked. And Auntie Peggy was so warm and welcoming, though she never did stop talking. She was still a good-looking woman in 1974.'

'I loved them both, just as I loved Auntie Susie. But my father and Susie never hit it off. I knew those tensions throughout my teenage years. What had once been a battle over my mother became a battle over me. It was Susie apparently who nearly "ruined it". He told me how she couldn't stop interfering. Apparently she ticked him off at their very first meeting: "I hope you won't be messing my sister around again. You've already hurt her feelings enough blowing hot and cold"... or something like that. I remember Dad telling me, "I nearly packed up my bags there and then and headed back to London."'

The next day *we* head back to London. It's now time to try and reconstruct it all, put together all the fragments. There are the letters themselves, the photographs, theirs and ours, the family history from Bonny and the family tree from Sue. There is my diary of the trip and there are Lawrence's poems. There's the archival research from all the libraries, the photograph of Cosmo's Strand Café sent by his grandson, Mark Matea, and there are the objects: the boomerang, the gold watch made by Pearce and Sons with 'G. P. Landsborough 94 Fitzwilliam Street' engraved on the back, the red dress, the diamond ring and, perhaps most important of all, that little green address book. I flick though it yet again, hoping for some new discovery. There it is on the second page, scribbled down in pencil:

Arncliffe
The Falcon

*

The letters came more frequently after Jack and Trudie's holiday in the Dales and their decision to marry. I won't describe it as an engagement as they didn't. My mother didn't have an engagement ring from Jack. She wore the small four-diamond ring that she had inherited from her Aunt Susan, Marie's sister, whose fiancé had died in the first war. The wedding ring itself was difficult enough to find, despite her uncle owning the jewellery store Pearce and Sons in Huddersfield.

Susie took me to a pawn shop to try and find a 22 carat gold ring but they were all too big for my small finger. I shall have to choose the 9 carat one that Uncle Henry has in the shop.

Finding household items for their new life was a challenge in a time where everything was in short supply:

Jack my dearest,
I'm looking at second hand furniture rather than utility stuff. Susie and I saw a beautiful desk yesterday. It is oak with a carved lid.

And

Peggy is buying us a dinner wagon, very useful as it turns into a card table.

Trying to find suitable material for attractive blackout curtains, finding sheets and domestic appliances took a lot of management. Even Jack reported on the success of getting hold of an electric kettle. The letters don't suggest excitement about the wedding itself. The excitement is about their new life together:

My Darling Trudie
What a lovely letter you wrote on Monday. I was thrilled at the delightful presents and things your letter mentioned. It will be wonderful to have a little home with these things around and I thought when I finish school this after-noon how perfect it would be if I could go home to you and have

a nice little after-noon tea together! Still these days will come. What I did do on the way home was investigate the Earl's Court area. I think a small flat there might suit us perfectly. Sidney has promised to give me some tips about flats. He worked in an estate agents before he joined up to work for ENSOR.

Trudie's last letter was written on 16 July 1943. It described the rush at the end of term to get Sports Day done, to pack up the year, and for Trudie to pack up her own things for the last time, including the jug and glasses given to her by poor Miss Milner. By this time Jack had found the flat in Earl's Court and hired the decorators:

Do you think the housekeeper at the flat would be able to scrub the floors for us after the decorations have finished? And we need curtain rods fixed before the decorating starts.

My mother was always so practical, unlike my father. Trudie ends the letter:

Only a week today, my dearest, then no more good-byes.

*

Although I am a great one for clearing out, I've never managed to throw away the red wedding dress and the little mock-leopard-skin jacket with the padded shoulders. The dress has a few tiny moth holes despite being wrapped up with moth balls, and the silk lining of the jacket has been eaten away.

When I was young I would ask my mother why she hadn't got married in white. She'd always say, 'It was during the war.' She gave the same answer to the question about church. I was never totally satisfied. The photo of Auntie Peggy and Uncle Henry, who also got married during the war, in 1942, showed Uncle Henry looking magnificent in a top hat and tails, and Auntie Peggy in a white dress and a long flowing veil that spread around her in a pool of lace. There were the three bridesmaids, my mother, Auntie Joyce and the little girl all dressed up in white. My mother didn't have one bridesmaid, not even Auntie Susie. I felt cheated. One of my great ambitions was to be a bridesmaid, like the little girl in the photograph. The red dress was a great disappointment to me.

Later, after my mother died, I would try it on with the jacket and the little cloche hat which was made of the same red crêpe. I loved picking out the dresses that were left at her end of the wardrobe. Auntie Susie, petite like her sister, had taken some of my mother's clothes but left the things that she knew she wouldn't wear. She was a smart, plain dresser, not into 'prettiness', and maybe she was even thinking that I would wear them one day. I have no idea what happened to the black velvet evening dress or the blue floral silk, but the red dress survived. It came back into fashion in the early 1970s and actually fitted me for a short period while I was very slim. I wore the dress and jacket on my first meeting with Lawrence's brother Philip and his wife, Gwyneth. They must have thought I was very 'hippy' as I wore the whole outfit with high leather boots!

*

Trudie wore the red crêpe dress, with her padded-shouldered mock-leopard-skin jacket and her cloche hat one day at the end of July 1943. I have no idea what Jack wore as there are no photographs. According to Trudie's last letter, the arrangements were simple: registry office marriage at 10.30, coffee and cake with the immediate Landsborough family, then off on the train south at 12 for their 'honeymoon'.

Whether it was just the war or whether it was Jack's desire to avoid fuss I have no idea. I rather tend to think Jack used the 'present times' as his excuse to miss a Landsborough wedding.

After a short honeymoon they set up home in the flat in Earl's Court, in Pennywern Road. Though I think I once knew the number it's forgotten now. I remember driving past the block of red mansion flats when I was a little girl and we were on our way to Grannie Annie's in Dulwich. Mummy said, 'That's where Daddy and I lived during the war, when we first got married.' There is one story that my mother told me about the flat that I have not forgotten.

It was very soon after we were married. The bombs started again. The 'little Blitz' they called it. It was a Saturday and we'd just popped out for a stroll. We heard the sirens and ran for shelter. When we got back home we discovered the block of flats had been damaged. Our flat was a complete mess as the ceiling had fallen in. Imagine if we had been there. I couldn't bear to think about it at the time. As we cleared up we came upon something we didn't recognize at all. It was a circular piece of grey material. We both realised at the same moment what it was. It was Daddy's trilby hat completely flattened. What luck or chance took us out that after-noon? After all we were only just somewhere round the corner.

CHAPTER 14 – Memory

MY MOTHER TAUGHT ME TO REMEMBER. From when I was small we would recite together what presents I'd had for my previous birthdays: a red pedal car when I was three, a teddy bear when I was four, a doll's house when I was five, a two-wheeler bike when I was six, and so on. We'd remember where we'd gone for our summer holiday and when we'd last been visited by Auntie Susie or Grannie Annie. She encouraged me to remember by heart nursery rhymes, songs and poems. I can still recite much of Lewis Carroll and *A Child's Garden of Verse*. Yet now in the twenty-first century we are told by the cutting-edge scientists that there is no such thing as memory, it is more a dynamic, inexact, imaginative process, with each act of remembering or retelling changing the memory itself. All memory is reconstruction. I have used these 'inexact' memories, these 'reconstructions' in the search for my mother and my father, stimulated by research and archives, visits, photographs, objects and, most importantly, letters. Those letters from my grandmother to her sister Winnie that I'd hidden away in the trunk tie in exactly with my memories, but there are details too that I had completely forgotten, like being very ill with tonsillitis:

Dear Old Win,
I don't know what to say about messing up the week-end for you. I tried to get you on the phone but couldn't.

Jennifer has been very ill with tonsillitis. I couldn't possibly leave Jack in the lurch, he has been so poorly himself and little Jennifer is naturally missing her mother.

She writes in an earlier letter:

The children are still now the greatest problem. Jennifer is away most of the time with her little friend, Jill. Peter is sad and forlorn. They tackle it in different ways. Peter buries himself in his school work while Jennifer is more open and liable to tears. She realises I think that her mother will never come home but she still asks to visit. She talks about the last time she saw her mother which is almost three months ago now. She keeps saying 'I promised Mummy I'd visit again.' She doesn't realise of course that her mother has forgotten all about her, would not recognize her own children.

It is Easter Day, late March 1959. Peter and I are staying at Auntie Vy's. I am thrilled with my beautiful Easter egg, which Mummy has had iced especially for me. It has been our bargain. I have set my heart on an enormous Easter egg to rival the one Jill Brisbourne had last year. I have given up my weekly packet of Cadbury's milk chocolate finger biscuits for a whole term in exchange for this. And here it is! The top of the egg is covered with little pink rosebuds and green leaves and there is pink writing which says: 'For dearest Jennifer love from Mummy and Daddy'. I am determined not to cry in front of Michael and Peter. Michael teases me and says, 'It's almost as big as you.' Inside the egg are lots of tiny little chocolate finger biscuits. Auntie Vy promises to take us to visit Mummy this very afternoon and I will wrap up some egg to take for her.

She is lying in the end bed of the ward and not like mummy any more. Her beautiful coiffed silver-white hair is all long and straggly and loose. Everything is white: her hair, her face, her nightgown, the bed, the pillows, the sheets. I look at her looking at Peter and part of me knows the truth. I offer the little bit of Easter egg in its silver paper and she smiles gently and looks away. When we leave I look back and say, 'I'll see you again very soon, Mummy, I promise.'

I have kept this memory alive. The scientist or therapist might say it is because I needed to, that it's not necessarily how it was, that others would remember the same event differently. But I have no one to check with any more.

And Jack, what did he keep alive from this terrible time? He rarely talked in detail about it. He would say that, as the tumour progressed, she stopped being the Trudie he knew and, of course, she stopped 'knowing' him. There is one conversation I do remember clearly which took place near the end of Jack's life.

He has moved to the Tottenham flat and I call in each day on my way home from Langdon School in East Ham. I let myself in and enter the living room at the front, where I know he'll be sitting in his big chair, reading or dozing or daydreaming.

'I've been thinking, Jen,' he says, 'about life and such.'

'What's new?' I think to myself as I put the kettle on. I don't want to listen again to his anxieties about my brother, it just upsets us both. But when I take in the tea

I say, 'Tell me, Dad, what have you been thinking about?'

'It's your mother. If only I'd insisted she saw the doctor as soon as she started the headaches. I even felt there was something wrong back in the summer before, you know, Jen, when we went to Italy?'

'Why, Dad?' I remember that holiday with fondness. Our last summer holiday all together. My mother, to my nine-year-old eyes, had seemed just Mummy.

'She was always so good at planning and remembering every detail. Something had changed. She just wasn't her usual self. She'd forget things – Trudie, whose memory I had always relied on. We had to drive back at one point to pick up Peter's asthma inhaler, left in a hotel bedroom. It was really strange for her to forget that.'

He pauses, then turns to me and says, 'I really fell in love with Trudie once we were married. I wasted so much time before through my own stupidity. I thought we'd grow old together, I thought we'd have years together.'

I felt a little disappointed back then. I must have wanted revelations of passion at Pago Pago. At twenty-four love was the great unobtainable, the hunt for Mr Darcy, the passion of Ursula and Birkin, the love of Anna for Vronsky. I wasn't so unlike that young Jack whom I have now discovered: wanting what I couldn't have, seeking the beautiful, imagining the romantic. I wish I could talk to him now and say, 'Dad, I'm really sorry you missed out on those years, those later years when you would have known each other so well, have shared so much. All those years you both should have had, you and Trudie.'

I see them now on the square at Bormes-Les-Mimosas, that pretty hill village close to Toulon, in the south of France, where we stayed in the summer of 1957, less than two years before my mother died. Trudie is wearing a strapless turquoise dress; she is tanned and looks sparkling, probably because she's wearing more make-up than usual. Jack is wearing a light cream summer jacket. I notice how Peter is staring at them too, from our corner right on the edge of the square. We both feel strangely cut out of our parents' world. We are used to being the centre of their attention. But as they dance and dance it is as if they have forgotten all about us. It is just the two of them waltzing in the square while we look on unnoticed.

Peter and Jennifer on Holiday in France, 1957

'When I was still "Somewhere Round the Corner"'

ACKNOWLEDGEMENTS

Writing Groups: Barbara Jenkins and Nicolette Laird Paddington in Trinidad, Barbara Bleiman and Wendy Weinstock in London.

Research:

UK: Susan Black (née Landsborough) for finding and sending Trudie's letters; South Place Ethical Society library; Bonny Landsborough on family archive; Pat Rigg and Jane McIntosh and those at Real Holidays for journey planning.

Sri Lanka: Romesh and Helen Gunesekera

Western Australia: The Lange family; South Terrace Primary School, Freemantle; The museum and tourist office at Nanup; The Residency Museum, The library, and Yorke Street Primary School and Teachers' Centre at Albany; Mark Manea (Spero's grandson).

New Zealand: The library Rotorua; the tourist office Taumarunui; the library New Plymouth; Rod and Margot Mckay; Zelda Mckay; the library Dunedin; Stuart Landsborough and Puzzling World.

Toulon: Annie Griffiths

Reading manuscript with editorial advice Barbara Bleiman, Carol Raphael, Alan Mahar (founder Tindal Street Press), Andrew Hewson (Johnson and Alcock Literary Agency), and all other friends who have read various drafts.

Copy-editing Lesley Levine

Enhancement of photographs Penny Bowen and Eugene McConville

Map Pat Rigg

Design and Layout Glenda Pattenden

Cover Design Andy Dark

Twelve Acre Publishing Mike Green